Exam AI-1∪∠

Designing and Implementing a Microsoft Azure AI Solution

Latest and Exclusive Practice tests

So, if you're looking to test your knowledge, and practice the real exam questions, you are on the right place.

This New Book contains the Latest Questions, Detailed and Exclusive Explanation + References.

Our book covers all topics included in the AI-102 exam.

The Microsoft Azure AI-102 exam encompasses 40-60 questions, featuring diverse formats such as multiple-choice questions, scenario-based single-answer questions, arrange-in-correct-sequence type questions, mark review, drag & drop questions, and others.

This book will undergo periodic updates to align with the skills essential for successfully passing the official exam.

PRACTICE TEST I

1) DRAG DROP:

You manage 100 chatbots, each equipped with its own Language Understanding model. It is a common task to regularly incorporate identical phrases into each of these models.

You are required to update the Language Understanding models programmatically to incorporate the new phrases.

How should you complete the code?

To respond, arrange the suitable values into the correct targets [1] and [2].

Each value can be utilized once, more than once, or not at all.

Select and Place:

<u>Values:</u>

a. AddPhraseListAsync

b. Phraselist

c. PhraselistCreateObject

d. Phrases

e. SavePhraselistAsync

f. UploadPhraselistAsync

Answer area:

```
var phraselistId = await client.Features. [1]
(appId, versionId, new [2]
{
    EnabledForAllModels = false,
    IsExchangeable = true,
    Name = "PL1",
    Phrases = "item1,item2,item3,item4,item5"

});
```

2) DRAG DROP:

You intend to utilize an application for Language Understanding called app1, deployed within a container. The development of app1 utilized a Language Understanding authoring resource named lu1, and it possesses the versions outlined in the table below.

Version	Trained date	Published date
V1.2	None	None
V1.1	2020-10-01	None
V1.0	2020-09-01	2020-09-15

To produce a container utilizing the most recent deployable version of app1, what are the three sequential actions you should take?

To answer, choose the appropriate actions from the list of actions to the answer area and arrange them in the correct order.

Select and Place:

Actions:

a. Run a container that has version set as an environment variable.

b. Export the model by using the Export as JSON option.

c. Select v1.1 of app1.

d. Run a container and mount the model file.

e. Select v1.0 of app1.

f. Export the model by using the Export for containers (GZIP) option.

g. Select v1.2 pf app1.

Answer area:

1)...

2)...

3)...

3) You are tasked with constructing a chatbot that fulfills the following criteria:

- Supports chit-chat, knowledge base, and multilingual models
- Conducts sentiment analysis on user messages
- Automatically selects the most suitable language model

What components should you incorporate into the chatbot?

A. QnA Maker, Language Understanding, and Dispatch

B. Translator, Speech, and Dispatch

C. Language Understanding, Text Analytics, and QnA Maker

D. Text Analytics, Translator, and Dispatch

4) Your organization aims to streamline the process of logging

receipts in expense reports, with all receipts being in English. The objective is to extract key information from the receipts, such as the vendor and transaction total, while minimizing development effort.

Which Azure service should be employed for this purpose?

A. Custom Vision

B. Personalizer

C. Form Recognizer

D. Computer Vision

5) HOTSPOT:

You are required to establish a new resource to conduct sentiment analysis and optical character recognition (OCR). The solution needs to adhere to the following criteria:

- Employ a single key and endpoint for accessing multiple services.
- Aggregate billing for prospective services that may be utilized in the future.
- Be capable of accommodating the use of Computer Vision at a later stage.

To address this, choose the correct options [1] and [2] in the provided answer area to complete the HTTP request for creating the new resource.

Hot Area:

Answer area:

[1] `https://management.azure.com/subscriptions/xxxxxxxx-xxxx-`

```
XXXX-XXXX-
XXXXXXXXXXXX/resourceGroups/RG1/providers/Microsoft.CognitiveServices/
accounts/CS1?api-version=2017-04-18
{
  "location": "West US",
  "kind": " [2]

  "sku": {
    "name": "S0"

  },
  "properties": {},
  "identity": {
    "type": "SystemAssigned"

  }
}
```

[1] a. PATCH

    b. POST

    c. PUT

[2] a. CognitiveServices

    b. ComputerVision

    c. TextAnalytics

6) As you develop a new sales system that processes video and text from a public-facing website, you aim to ensure equitable results regardless of the user's location or background.

Which two responsible AI principles offer guidance for meeting these monitoring requirements? Each accurate selection contributes to the solution.

A. Transparency

B. Fairness

C. Inclusiveness

D. Reliability and Safety

E. Privacy and Security

7) DRAG DROP:

You are preparing to deploy containerized versions of the Anomaly Detector API on local devices for testing and in on-premises datacenters. The objective is to ensure that these containerized deployments satisfy the following conditions:

Prevent the storage of billing and API information in the command-line histories of the devices running the container.

Manage access to the container images through the utilization of Azure Role-Based Access Control (Azure RBAC).

Which four actions should you perform in sequence?

To answer, choose the appropriate actions from the list of actions to the answer area and arrange them in the correct order.

Select and Place:

Actions:

a. Create a custom Dockerfile.

b. Pull the anomaly Detector container image.

c. Distribute a Docker run script.

d. Push the image to an Azure container registry.

e. Build the image.

f. Push the image to Docker Hub.

Answer area:

1)...

2)...

3)..

4)..

8) HOTSPOT:

You intend to deploy a containerized version of an Azure Cognitive Services service dedicated to text analysis. After setting-up https://contoso.cognitiveservices.azure.com as the endpoint URI and obtaining the latest version of the Text Analytics Sentiment Analysis container, your task is to execute the container on an Azure virtual machine using Docker.

How should you complete the command? To answer, choose the appropriate options in the answer area.

Hot area:

1) docker run --rm -it -p 5000:5000 --memory 8g --cpus 1 \

a. https://contoso.blob.core.windows.net

 b. https://contoso.cognitiveservices.azure.com

c. mcr.microsoft.com/azure-cognitive-services/textanalytics/keyphrase

 d. mcr.microsoft.com/azure-cognitive-services/textanalytics/sentiment

\

Eula =accept \

2) Billing=

 a. https://contoso.blob.core.windows.net

b. https://contoso.cognitiveservices.azure.com

c. mcr.microsoft.com/azure-cognitive-services/textanalytics/keyphrase

d. mcr.microsoft.com/azure-cognitive-services/textanalytics/ sentiment

\

ApiKey=xxxxxxxxxxxxxxxxxxxx

9) You have the following C# method for creating Azure Cognitive Services resources programmatically.

```
static void create_resource(CognitiveServicesManagementClient client, string
resource_name, string kind, string account_tier, string location)
{
  CognitiveServicesAccount parameters =
      new CognitiveServicesAccount(null, null, kind, location, resource_name,
new CognitiveServicesAccountProperties(), new Sku(account_tier));
  var result = client.Accounts.Create(resource_group_name, account_tier,
parameters);
}
```

You need to call the method to create a free Azure resource in the West US Azure region. The resource will be used to generate captions of images automatically.

Which code should you use?

A. create_resource(client, "res1", "ComputerVision", "F0", "westus")

B. create_resource(client, "res1", "CustomVision.Prediction", "F0", "westus")

C. create_resource(client, "res1", "ComputerVision", "S0", "westus")

D. create_resource(client, "res1", "CustomVision.Prediction", "S0", "westus")

10) After successfully executing the provided HTTP request:

POST   https://management.azure.com/ subscriptions/18c51a87-3a69-47a8-aedc-a54745f708a1/

resourceGroups/RG1/providers/Microsoft.CognitiveServices/ accounts/contoso1/regenerateKey?api-version=2017-04-18

Body: {"keyName": "Key2"}

What is the outcome of the request?

A. Azure Cognitive Services key was generated in Azure Key Vault.

B. A new query key was generated.

C. The primary and secondary subscription keys were rotated.

D. The secondary subscription key was reset.

11) You build a custom Form Recognizer model.
You receive sample files to use for training the model as shown in the following table.

Name	Type	Size
File1	PDF	20 MB
File2	MP4	100 MB
File3	JPG	20 MB
File4	PDF	100 MB
File5	GIF	1 MB
File6	JPG	40 MB

Which three files can you use to train the model?

Each correct answer presents a complete solution.

A. File1

B. File2

C. File3

D. File4

E. File5

F. File6

12) A customer is utilizing Azure Cognitive Search and intends to implement server-side encryption with customer-managed keys (CMK) stored in Azure.

What are three outcomes of this planned change?

Each correct response represents a comprehensive solution.

A. The index size will increase.

B. Query times will increase.

C. A self-signed X.509 certificate is required.

D. The index size will decrease.

E. Query times will decrease.

F. Azure Key Vault is required.

13) As you work on a new sales system that processes video and text from a public-facing website, you aim to inform users about the processing of their data.

Which responsible AI principle does this action align with?

A. Transparency

B. Fairness

C. Inclusiveness

D. Reliability and Safety

14) This question is one of a set of questions sharing a common scenario. Each question in the set presents a distinct solution that could potentially meet the specified objectives. Some sets may have more than one valid solution, while others may not have a correct solution.

You are developing a web app, app1, hosted on an Azure virtual machine named vm1, which is part of an Azure virtual network named vnet1.

You intend to establish a new Azure Cognitive Search service named service1. Your objective is to enable direct connectivity from app1 to service1, eliminating the need to route traffic over the public internet.

Solution: You deploy service1 and a public endpoint to a new virtual network, and you configure Azure Private Link.

Does this meet the goal?

A. Yes

B. No

15) This question is one of a set of questions sharing a common scenario. Each question in the set presents a distinct solution that could potentially meet the specified objectives. Some sets may have more than one valid solution, while others may not have a correct solution.

You are developing a web app, app1, hosted on an Azure virtual machine named vm1, which is part of an Azure virtual network named vnet1.

You intend to establish a new Azure Cognitive Search service named service1. Your objective is to enable direct connectivity from app1 to service1, eliminating the need to route traffic over the public internet.

Solution: You deploy service1 and a public endpoint, and you configure an IP firewall rule.

Does this meet the goal?

A. Yes

B. No

16) This question is one of a set of questions sharing a common scenario. Each question in the set presents a distinct solution that could potentially meet the specified objectives. Some sets may have more than one valid solution, while others may not have a correct solution.

You are developing a web app, app1, hosted on an Azure virtual machine named vm1, which is part of an Azure virtual network named vnet1.

You intend to establish a new Azure Cognitive Search service named service1. Your objective is to enable direct connectivity from app1 to service1, eliminating the need to route traffic over the public internet.

Is the following solution adequate to achieve the goal: Deploying service1 with a public endpoint and configuring a network security group (NSG) for vnet1?

A. Yes

B. No

17) You plan to perform predictive maintenance. You gather IoT sensor data from 100 industrial machines over a year, with each machine having 50 sensors generating data at one-minute intervals. In total, there are 5,000 time series datasets. Your goal is to detect unusual values in each time series to aid in predicting machinery failures.

Which Azure service is suitable for this task?

A. Anomaly Detector

B. Cognitive Search

C. Form Recognizer

D. Custom Vision

18) HOTSPOT:

You are working on a streaming Speech to Text solution that will utilize the Speech SDK and MP3 encoding.

You need to develop a method to convert speech to text for streaming MP3 data.

How should you complete the code?

To answer, choose the appropriate options in the answer area.

Hot area:

Answer area:

```
var audioformat =    [1]      (AudioStreamContainerFormat.MP3);

var speechConfig = SpeechConfig.FromSubscription
("18c51a87-3a69-47a8-aedc-a54745f708a1", "westus");

var audioConfig = AudioConfig.FromStreamInput(pushStream, audioFormat);

using (var recognizer = new     [2]      (speechConfig, audioConfig))
 {

 var result = await recognizer.RecognizeOnceAsync();

 var text = result.Text;

 }
```

[1]

a. AdioConfig.SetProperty

b. AudioStreamFormat.GetCompressedFormat

c. AudioStreamFormat.GetWaveFormatPCM

c. PullAudioInputStream

[2]

a. KeywordRecognizer

b. SpeakerRecognizer

c. SpeechRecognizer

d. SpeechSynthesizer

19) HOTSPOT:

You are creating an online training solution for remote learners, and your company has observed that some learners tend to leave their desks for extended periods or become distracted during the training. Your task is to utilize the video and audio feeds from each learner's computer to determine their presence and attention levels. The solution should

minimize development effort and accurately identify each learner.

Which Azure Cognitive Services service should you use for each requirement?

To answer, choose the appropriate options in the answer area.

Hot area:

Answer area:

1) From a learner's video feed, verify whether the learner is present:

a. Face

b. Speech

c. Test Analytics

2) From learner's facial expression in the video feed, verify whether the learner is paying attention:

a. Face

b. Speech

c. Test Analytics

3) From learner's audio feed, detect whether the learner is talking:

 a. Face

b. Speech

c. Test Analytics

20) When provisioning a QnA Maker service in a new resource group named RG1.

In RG1, you create an App Service plan named AP1.

Which two Azure resources are automatically created in RG1 when you provision the QnA Maker service?

Each correct answer contributes to the solution.

A. Language Understanding

B. Azure SQL Database

C. Azure Storage

D. Azure Cognitive Search

E. Azure App Service

21) You're establishing a language model using the Language Understanding (classic) service, and you've set up a new Language Understanding (classic) resource. How can you incorporate additional contributors to this resource?

A. a conditional access policy in Azure Active Directory (Azure AD).

B. the Access control (IAM) page for the authoring resources in the Azure portal.

C. the Access control (IAM) page for the prediction resources in the Azure portal.

22) This question is part of a series featuring a consistent scenario. Each question within the series offers a distinct solution that could potentially fulfill the specified objectives. Some sets of questions may have multiple correct solutions, while others might not have a valid solution.

You possess an Azure Cognitive Search service, and over the

last 12 months, the volume of search queries has consistently risen. Upon investigation, you find that certain search query requests to the Cognitive Search service are experiencing throttling. Your objective is to minimize the chances of search query requests being throttled.

Solution: You migrate to a Cognitive Search service that uses a higher tier.

Does this meet the goal?

A. Yes

B. No

23) DRAG DROP:

To build an automated call handling system capable of responding to callers in their preferred language (French and English), match each requirement with the appropriate Azure Cognitive Services service.

Drag each service to the correct requirement; each service may be used once, more than once, or not at all.

Select and Place:

Services:

a. Speaker Recognition

b. Speech to Text

c. Text Analytics

d. Text to Speech

e. Translator

Answer area:

1) Detect the incoming language: ....

2) Respond in the callers' own language: ......

24) You have receipts available via a URL and aim to extract data from them using Form Recognizer and the SDK. The requirement is to utilize a prebuilt model. Which client and method combination should you employ?

A. Leverage the FormRecognizerClient client and the StartRecognizeContentFromUri method.

B. Utilize the FormTrainingClient client and the StartRecognizeContentFromUri method.

C. Employ the FormRecognizerClient client and the StartRecognizeReceiptsFromUri method.

D. Use the FormTrainingClient client and the StartRecognizeReceiptsFromUri method.

25) You possess a collection of 50,000 scanned documents containing text and intend to make the text accessible through Azure Cognitive Search. To set up an enrichment pipeline for optical character recognition (OCR) and text analytics while minimizing costs, what should you associate with the skillset?

A. Connect a new Computer Vision resource.

B. Link a free (Limited enrichments) Cognitive Services resource.

C. Associate an Azure Machine Learning Designer pipeline.

D. Attach a new Cognitive Services resource utilizing the S0 pricing tier.

26) This question is part of a series featuring a consistent scenario. Each question within the series provides a distinct solution that could potentially fulfill the specified objectives. Some sets of questions may have multiple correct solutions, while others might not have a valid solution.

You possess an Azure Cognitive Search service, and over the last 12 months, the volume of search queries has consistently risen. Upon investigation, you find that certain search query requests to the Cognitive Search service are experiencing throttling. Your objective is to minimize the chances of search query requests being throttled.

Solution: You add indexes.

Does this meet the goal?

A. Yes

B. No

27) This question is part of a series featuring a consistent scenario. Each question within the series provides a distinct solution that could potentially fulfill the specified objectives. Some sets of questions may have multiple correct solutions, while others might not have a valid solution.

You possess an Azure Cognitive Search service, and over the last 12 months, the volume of search queries has consistently risen. Upon investigation, you find that certain search query requests to the Cognitive Search service are experiencing throttling. Your objective is to minimize the chances of search query requests being throttled.

Solution: You enable customer-managed key (CMK) encryption.

Does this meet the goal?

A. Yes

B. No

28) This question is part of a series featuring a consistent scenario. Each question within the series provides a distinct solution that could potentially fulfill the specified objectives. Some sets of questions may have multiple correct solutions, while others might not have a valid solution.

You've established a web app named app1 running on an Azure virtual machine (vm1) within an Azure virtual network named vnet1. Your intention is to set up a new Azure Cognitive Search service called service1. Your goal is to enable a direct connection from app1 to service1 without routing traffic through the public internet.

Solution: You deploy service1 and a private endpoint to vnet1.

Does this meet the goal?

A. Yes

B. No

29) You possess a Language Understanding resource named lu1. You've developed and deployed an Azure bot named bot1 that utilizes lu1. To align bot1 with the Microsoft responsible AI principle of inclusiveness, what action should you take?

A. Implement authentication for bot1.

B. Enable active learning for lu1.

C. Host lu1 in a container.

D. Integrate Direct Line Speech into bot1.

30) HOTSPOT:

You are developing an application responsible for handling incoming email and direct messages, directing them to either French or English language support teams. Which Azure Cognitive Services API should you employ? Choose the correct options in the provided answer area.

Hot area:

Answer area:

https://.............[1]..........[2].....................

Options:

[1]

a. api.cognitive.microsofttranslator.com

b. eastus.api.cognitive.microsoft.com

c. portal.azure.com

[2]

a. /text/analytics/v3.1/entities/recognition/general

b. /text/analytics/v3.1/languages

c. /translator/text/v3.0/translate?to=en

d. /translator/text/v3.0/translate?to=fr

31) You have an Azure Cognitive Search instance that indexes purchase orders using Form Recognizer. To analyze

the extracted information with Microsoft Power BI while minimizing development effort, what should you incorporate into the indexer?

A. a projection group

B. a table projection

C. a file projection

D. an object projection

32) This question is part of a series featuring a consistent scenario. Each question within the series provides a distinct solution that could potentially fulfill the specified objectives. Some sets of questions may have multiple correct solutions, while others might not have a valid solution.

You possess an Azure Cognitive Search service, and over the last 12 months, the volume of search queries has consistently risen. Upon investigation, you find that certain search query requests to the Cognitive Search service are experiencing throttling. Your objective is to minimize the chances of search query requests being throttled.

Solution: You add replicas.

Does this meet the goal?

A. Yes

B. No

33) HOTSPOT:

You have an Azure Cognitive Search resource named Search1 that multiple apps use. To enhance security, you must fulfill

the following criteria:

Restrict internet access to Search1.

Control each app's access to specific queries.

What actions should you take?

Choose the correct options in the answer area.

Answer area:

1) To prevent access from the internet:

a. Configure an IP firewall

b. Create a private endpoint

c. Use Azure roles

2) To limit access to queries:

a. Create a private endpoint

b. Use Azure roles

c. Use key authentication

34) You are developing a solution to identify anomalies in sensor data from the past 24 hours. You must ensure that the entire dataset is simultaneously scanned for anomalies.

What type of detection should you employ?

A. batch

B. streaming

C. change points

35) DRAG DROP:

As you develop an application to scan confidential documents and utilize the Language service to analyze their contents, you provision an Azure Cognitive Services resource.

To ensure that the app can make requests to the Language service endpoint while keeping confidential documents on-premises, arrange the following three actions in the correct order by moving them from the list to the answer area.

Actions:

a. Run the container and specify an App ID and Client Secret.

b. Provision an on-premises Kubernetes cluster that is isolated from the internet.

c. Pull an image from the Microsoft Container Registry (MCR).

d. Run the container and specify an API key and the Endpoint URL of the Cognitive Services resource.

e. Provision an on-premises Kubernetes cluster that has internet connectivity.

f. Pull an image from Docker Hub.

g. Provision an Azure Kubernetes Service (AKS) resource.

Answer area:

1)...

2)...

3)...

36) HOTSPOT:

In your Azure subscription with the specified configurations (Subscription ID: 8d3591aa-96b8-4737-ad09-00f9b1ed35ad, Tenant ID: 3edfe572-cb54-3ced-ae12-c5c177f39a12)

You intend to create a resource for performing sentiment analysis and optical character recognition (OCR) using an HTTP request. The requirement is to utilize a single key and endpoint.

Complete the request by selecting the appropriate options in the answer area.

Answer area:

https://management.azure.com/[1]/resourceGroups/ OCRProject/providers/[2]/accounts/CS1?api-version-2021-10-01

[1]

a. subscriptions/3edfe572-cb54-3ced-ae12-c5c177139a12

b. subscriptions/8d3591aa-96b8-4737-ad09-00f9b1ed35ad

c. tenant/3edfe572-cb54-3ced-ae12-c5c177f39a12

d. tenant/8d3591aa-96b8-4737-ad09-00f9b1ed35ad

[2]

a. Microsoft.ApiManagement

b. Microsoft.CognitiveServices

c. Microsoft.ContainerService

d. Microsoft.KeyVault

37) You operate a factory producing food products and require a monitoring solution for staff compliance with personal

protective equipment (PPE) requirements. The solution must fulfill the following criteria:

- Detect staff members who have removed masks or safety glasses.
- Conduct a compliance check every 15 minutes.
- Minimize development effort.
- Minimize costs.

Which service should you utilize?

A. Face

B. Computer Vision

C. Azure Video Analyzer for Media (formerly Video Indexer)

38) You have an Azure Cognitive Search solution and a set of blog posts with a category field. Index the posts to fulfill the following criteria:

- Incorporate the category field in the search results.
- Allow users to search for words within the category field.
- Enable users to perform drill-down filtering based on category.

Which index attributes should you configure for the category field?

A. searchable, sortable, and retrievable.

B. searchable, facetable, and retrievable.

C. retrievable, filterable, and sortable.

D. retrievable, facetable, and key.

39) In your Azure subscription, there's an Anomaly Detector resource. You've set up a Docker host server named Server1 in the on-premises network. To run an instance of the Anomaly Detector service on Server1, what parameter should be included in the docker run command?

A. Fluentd

B. Billing

C. Http Proxy

D. Mounts

40) As you develop an app utilizing the Speech service, you must enable authentication to the service using a Microsoft Azure Active Directory (Azure AD) token, which is a component of Microsoft Entra.

Identify the two actions that should be performed; each correct answer represents part of the solution.

A. Enable a virtual network service endpoint.

B. Configure a custom subdomain.

C. Request an X.509 certificate.

D. Create a private endpoint.

E. Create a Conditional Access policy.

41) You possess an application called App1, utilizing an S0 instance of Azure AI Document Intelligence, which extracts invoice data from PDF files. These PDF files can be up to 2 MB in size, each comprising a maximum of 10 pages.

Users report that App1 is unable to process some invoices.

You need to troubleshoot the issue.

What is a possible cause of the issue?

a. Some of the files are password protected.

b. Some of the files are too large.

c. Some of the files have too many pages.

d. The tier of the Azure AI Document Intelligence instance is insufficient.

42) You are developing a method that uses the Computer Vision client library. The method will perform optical character recognition (OCR) in images.

The method has the following code.

```
public static async Task ReadFileUrl(ComputerVisionClient client, string urlFile)
{
        const int numberOfCharsInOperationId = 36;

        var txtHeaders = await client.ReadAsync(urlFile, language: "en");

        string opLocation = textHeaders.OperationLocation;
        string operationId = opLocation.Substring(opLocation.Length -
numberOfCharsInOperationId);

        ReadOperationResult results;

        results = await client.GetReadResultAsync(Guid.Parse(operationId));

        var textUrlFileResults = results.AnalyzeResult.ReadResults;
        foreach (ReadResult page in textUrlFileResults)
        {
                foreach (Line line in page.Lines)
                {
                        Console.WriteLine(line.Text);
                }
        }
}
```

While conducting testing, you observe that the call to the GetReadResultAsync method happens before the read operation is finished.

To address this issue, you need to ensure that the

GetReadResultAsync method does not proceed until the read operation is complete.

Identify the two actions that should be taken; each correct answer represents part of the solution.

A. Remove the Guid.Parse(operationId) parameter.

B. Add code to verify the results.Status value.

C. Add code to verify the status of the txtHeaders.Status value.

D. Wrap the call to GetReadResultAsync within a loop that contains a delay.

43) You are developing an application that will extract text from scanned receipts.

You need to suggest a service to use, and the solution should minimize development effort.

What should you recommend?

a. Azure AI Vision

b. Azure AI Custom Vision

c. Azure AI Document Intelligence

d. Azure Machine Learning

44) You are developing an application intended for deployment on an edge device. The application will utilize Azure AI Custom Vision to analyze images of fruits.

You need to select a model domain for the app. The solution must support running the app without internet connectivity.

Which model should you use?

a. Compact domain

b. Food domain

c. General[A1] domain

d. General [A2] domain

45) You possess an application that examines images utilizing the Computer Vision API.

You need to configure the app to provide an output for users who are vision impaired. The solution must provide the output in complete sentences.

Which API call should you perform?

A. readInStreamAsync

B. analyzeImagesByDomainInStreamAsync

C. tagImageInStreamAsync

D. describeImageInStreamAsync

46) DRAG DROP:

You have a Custom Vision service project specializing in object detection. The project employs the General domain for classification and includes a trained model.

You need to export the model for use on a network that is disconnected from the internet.

Which three actions should you perform in sequence?

To answer, move the appropriate actions from the list of actions to the answer area and arrange them in the correct order.

Actions:

a. Change the classification type

b. Export the model

c. Retain the model

d. Change domains to General (compact)

e. Create new classification model

Answer area:

1)..

2)..

3)..

47) As you develop an AI solution leveraging Sentiment Analysis outcomes from surveys to determine bonuses for customer service staff, it's crucial to align with Microsoft's responsible AI principles.

What action should you take?

A. Integrate a human review and approval step before implementing decisions impacting the financial situation of the staff.

B. Factor in the Sentiment Analysis results specifically when surveys yield a low confidence score.

C. Incorporate all surveys, even those from customers who have requested the deletion of their account and data.

D. Share the raw survey data openly by publishing it to a centralized location and granting staff access to that location.

48) In your Azure subscription, there's a Language service resource named ta1 and a virtual network named vnet1. Your objective is to establish a configuration that allows access to ta1 exclusively for resources within vnet1.

What should you configure?

A. a network security group (NSG) for vnet1

B. Azure Firewall for vnet1

C. the virtual network settings for ta1

D. a Language service container for ta1

49) You are in the process of creating a monitoring system designed to assess data from engine sensors, including metrics like rotation speed, angle, temperature, and pressure.

The primary objective is to generate alerts in case of abnormal values.

What should you include in the solution?

A. Application Insights in Azure Monitor

B. metric alerts in Azure Monitor

C. Multivariate Anomaly Detection

D. Univariate Anomaly Detection

50) You possess an application called App1, utilizing an Azure Cognitive Services model to detect anomalies in a time series data stream. Your requirement is to operate App1 in a location with restricted connectivity, and the approach should be cost-

effective (The solution must minimize costs).

What option should you choose for running App1?

A. Azure Kubernetes Service (AKS)

B. Azure Container Instances

C. A Kubernetes cluster hosted in an Azure Stack Hub integrated system

D. The Docker Engine

51) You possess an application that forwards audio recordings from a call center to the speech-to-text functionality of Azure AI Services.

In the testing phase, you observe a high Word Error Rate (WER) with a significant number of substitution errors.

Your objective is to enhance the model and decrease the WER.

What should you add to the training data?

a. custom product and people names

b. overlapping speakers

c. people talking in the background

52) You are in the process of developing an application that enables users to generate notes through speech.

You must suggest the Azure AI Speech service model to utilize.

The solution must support noisy environments.

Which model should you recommend?

a. base

b. base with customizations

c. custom speech-to-text

d. default

53) You are constructing a custom translation model.

You must assess the accuracy of the translated text using a Bilingual Evaluation Understudy (BLEU) score.

Which scale is used for the score?

a. between 0 and 1

b. between 0 and 100

c. low, medium, and high

54) You are developing an application that utilizes Azure AI Services Document Translation. Your goal is to enhance the translation quality for documents uploaded by users.

What should you ask the users to include when they upload a document?

a. a summary

b. the file format

c. the source language

d. the writing style

55) You are constructing a custom model for Azure AI

Translator.

You must ensure that the model achieves a high-quality translation accuracy, as indicated by a Bilingual Evaluation Understudy (BLEU) score.

What is the minimum score range required?

a. 0 to 19

b. 20 to 39

c. 40 to 59

d. 60 to 79

e. 80 to 100

56) You are developing a model that utilizes Conversational Language Understanding (CLU).

What methods are available for training the model?

a. advanced, deterministic, and standard

b. advanced only

c. deterministic only

d. standard and advanced only

e. standard only

57) You are establishing an orchestration workflow for Language Understanding.

You must set up workflows for numerous languages.

The solution must minimize administrative effort.

What should you create for each language?

a. a new deployment

b. separate models

c. separate training jobs

d. separate workflow projects

58) You are developing a multilingual conversational app using Conversational Language Understanding (CLU), a component of the Azure AI Language service.

You have created a CLU model intended to support multiple languages.

Your goal is to enhance the model's performance while minimizing development efforts.

What should you do?

a. Add utterances for languages that are performing poorly in the model.

b. Configure the app to only query utterances in the language that was used to train the model.

c. Create separate projects for each language.

d. Train the model by using utterances in multiple languages and only query the model by using the project language.

59) You are configuring a question answering solution.

You execute the following API call and receive the following error.

"synonyms": [

```
{
  "alterations": [
    "fix problems",
    "troubleshoot",
    "#diagnostic",
    ]
},
...
```

You need to ensure that the API call executes successfully.

What should you do?

a. Modify the order of the synonyms.

b. Remove any question-and-answer pairs from the call.

c. Remove any special characters from the call.

60) You are developing a solution that utilizes the Azure AI Language question answering service.

You need to import FAQ documents for the solution.

What kinds of data will be extracted while importing documents in the process?

a. formatted text, URLs, and bulleted and numbered lists only

b. formatted text, URLs, images, and diagrams only

c. unformatted text, images, and diagrams only

d. unformatted text, numbered lists, and unstructured data only

ANSWERS AND EXPLANATION

1)

1. a. AddPhraseListAsync

2. c. PhraselistCreateObject

Example: Add phraselist feature -

var phraselistId = await client.Features.AddPhraseListAsync(appId, versionId, new PhraselistCreateObject

{

EnabledForAllModels = false,

IsExchangeable = true,

Name = "QuantityPhraselist",

Phrases = "few,more,extra"

});

Reference:

https://learn.microsoft.com/en-us/azure/cognitive-services/luis/client-libraries-rest-api?tabs=windows&pivots=programming-language-csharp#create-entities-for-the-app

https://learn.microsoft.com/en-us/azure/ai-services/luis/client-libraries-rest-api?tabs=windows&pivots=programming-language-csharp

// Add phraselist feature

var phraselistId = await client.Features.AddPhraseListAsync(appId, versionId, new PhraselistCreateObject

2) 1) c, 2) f, 3) d

1) c. Select v1.1 of app1.

Select the version 1.1 before exporting the model

2) f. Export the model by using the Export for containers (GZIP) option.

Export versioned app's package from LUIS portal

The versioned app's package is available from the Versions list page.

1. Sign on to the LUIS portal.

2. Select the app in the list.

3. Select Manage in the app's navigation bar.

4. Select Versions in the left navigation bar.

5. Select the checkbox to the left of the version name in the list.

6. Select the Export item from the contextual toolbar above the list.

7. Select Export for container (GZIP).

8. The package is downloaded from the browser.

3) d. Run a container and mount the model file.

Run the container, with the required input mount and billing settings.

"The Language Understanding (LUIS) container loads your trained or published Language Understanding model." Trained alone is deployable, v1.1

Reference:

https://learn.microsoft.com/en-us/azure/ai-services/luis/luis-container-howto?tabs=v3

https://docs.microsoft.com/en-us/azure/cognitive-services/luis/luis-container-howto

3) C

Language Understanding: An AI service that allows users to interact with your applications, bots, and IoT devices by using natural language.

QnA Maker is a cloud-based Natural Language Processing (NLP) service that allows you to create a natural conversational layer over your data. It is used to find the most appropriate answer for any input from your custom knowledge base (KB) of information.

Text Analytics: Mine insights in unstructured text using natural language processing (NLP) no machine learning expertise required. Gain a deeper understanding of customer opinions with sentiment analysis. The Language Detection feature of the Azure Text Analytics REST API evaluates text input

Incorrect Answers:

A, B, D: Dispatch uses sample utterances for each of your bot's different tasks (LUIS, QnA Maker, or custom), and builds a model that can be used to properly route your user's request to the right task, even across multiple bots.

Reference:

https://azure.microsoft.com/en-us/services/cognitive-services/text-analytics/

https://learn.microsoft.com/en-us/azure/cognitive-services/qnamaker/overview/overview

QnA Maker is commonly used to build conversational client applications, which include social media applications, chat bots, and speech-enabled desktop applications.

Supports chit-chat, - Language Understanding

knowledge base - Q&A Maker

sentiment analysis - text Analytics

4) C

To streamline the process of logging receipts in expense reports and extract top-level information like the vendor and transaction total, with a focus on minimizing development effort, you should use:

C. Form Recognizer

Explanation:

Form Recognizer is designed for extracting information from forms and documents, making it suitable for receipt analysis.

It can automatically identify and extract key information, such as vendor details and transaction total, from receipts.

Using Form Recognizer helps minimize the need for extensive custom development for receipt processing.

Option C, Form Recognizer, is the most appropriate choice for the specified requirements.

Azure Form Recognizer is a cloud-based Azure Applied AI Service that enables you to build intelligent document processing solutions. Massive amounts of data, spanning a wide variety of data types, are stored in forms and documents. Form Recognizer enables you to effectively manage the velocity at which data is collected and processed and is key to improved operations, informed data-driven decisions, and enlightened innovation.

Reference:

https://learn.microsoft.com/en-us/azure/applied-ai-services/ form-recognizer/overview?view=form-recog-3.0.0

5) 1) c, 2) a

1) c. PUT: puts a file or resource at a specific URI, and exactly at that URI.

If there's already a file or resource at that URI, PUT replaces that file or resource.

If there is no file or resource there, PUT creates one.

POST: POST sends data to a specific URI and expects the resource at that URI to handle the request.

Sample Request: PUT

https://management.azure.com/
subscriptions/00000000-0000-0000-0000-000000000000/
resourceGroups/test-rg/providers/

Microsoft.DeviceUpdate/accounts/contoso?api-
version=2020-03-01-preview

Incorrect Answers:

PATCH is for updates.

2) a. CognitiveServices

Microsoft Azure Cognitive Services provide us to use its pre-trained models for various Business Problems related to Machine Learning.

List of Different Services are:

∾ Decision

∾ Language (includes sentiment analysis)

∾ Speech

∾ Vision (includes OCR)

∾ Web Search

Reference:

https://docs.microsoft.com/en-us/rest/api/deviceupdate/
resourcemanager/accounts/create

https://www.analyticsvidhya.com/blog/2020/12/microsoft-
azure-cognitive-services-api-for-ai-development/

6) BC

To address the monitoring requirements for equitable results in your sales system, you should consider the following responsible AI principles:

B. Fairness

Fairness in AI involves ensuring that the system's outcomes are unbiased and do not favor or discriminate against any particular group of users based on factors like location or background.

C. Inclusiveness

Inclusiveness emphasizes the importance of designing AI systems that cater to diverse user populations, ensuring that the system is accessible and beneficial to users from various backgrounds and locations.

Explanation:

Fairness helps in preventing discriminatory outcomes, ensuring that the sales system treats all users impartially.

Inclusiveness ensures that the system is designed to accommodate users with different backgrounds and locations, contributing to a more equitable experience.

Therefore, the responsible AI principles that provide guidance for meeting the monitoring requirements are Fairness (B) and Inclusiveness (C).

Reference:

https://learn.microsoft.com/en-us/azure/cloud-adoption-framework/innovate/best-practices/trusted-ai#fairness

Fairness is a core ethical principle that all humans aim to understand and apply. This principle is even more important when AI systems are being developed. Key checks and balances need to make sure that the system's decisions don't discriminate or run a gender, race, sexual orientation, or religion bias toward a group or individual.

https://learn.microsoft.com/en-us/azure/cloud-adoption-framework/innovate/best-practices/trusted-ai#inclusiveness

Inclusiveness mandates that AI should consider all human races and experiences, and inclusive design practices can help developers to understand and address potential barriers that could unintentionally exclude people. Where possible, speech-to-text, text-to-speech, and visual recognition technology should be used to empower people with hearing, visual, and other impairments.

Fairness (equity) and Inclusiveness (regardless locations and backgrounds)

7) To ensure that the containerized deployments meet the specified conditions, perform the following actions in sequence:

a. Create a custom Dockerfile.

Create a custom Dockerfile to define the container's configuration, including security measures to prevent the storage of sensitive information in command-line histories.

e. Build the image.

Use the custom Dockerfile to build the container image with the specified configuration, ensuring that security measures are implemented during the build process.

d. Push the image to an Azure container registry.

Store the container image in an Azure container registry, which provides secure storage and management of container images.

c. Distribute a Docker run script.

Provide a Docker run script to facilitate the deployment of the containerized Anomaly Detector API, ensuring that it adheres to the security measures and prevents the storage of sensitive information.

Explanation:

Creating a custom Dockerfile (a) allows you to define the container's configuration, including security measures.

Building the image (e) ensures that the configured security measures are incorporated.

Pushing the image to an Azure container registry (d) provides secure storage for the container image.

Distributing a Docker run script (c) enables the deployment of the container with the specified security measures.

Note: The actions related to Docker Hub (f, b) are not necessary for the specific requirements mentioned in the scenario.

8) 1) c, 2) b

1. mcr.microsoft.com/azure-cognitive-services/textanalytics/sentiment

2. https://contoso.cognitiveservices.azure.com

To complete the Docker run command for deploying the Text Analytics Sentiment Analysis container on an Azure virtual machine, use the following options:

docker run --rm -it -p 5000:5000 --memory 8g --cpus 1 \

mcr.microsoft.com/azure-cognitive-services/textanalytics/sentiment \

--Eula accept \

--Billing https://contoso.cognitiveservices.azure.com \

--ApiKey xxxxxxxxxxxxxxxxxxxx

Explanation:

--rm: Automatically removes the container when it exits.

-it: Runs the container in interactive mode.

-p 5000:5000: Maps port 5000 on the host to port 5000 on the container.

--memory 8g: Specifies the maximum amount of memory the container can use.

--cpus 1: Limits the container to using 1 CPU.

mcr.microsoft.com/azure-cognitive-services/textanalytics/sentiment: Specifies the image to use for the container.

--Eula accept: Accepts the End User License Agreement (EULA) for the container.

--Billing https://contoso.cognitiveservices.azure.com: Sets the billing endpoint URI.

--ApiKey xxxxxxxxxxxxxxxxxxxx: Provides the API key for accessing the Text Analytics service.

This configuration ensures the proper execution of the containerized Text Analytics Sentiment Analysis service with the specified parameters.

Reference:

https://learn.microsoft.com/en-us/azure/cognitive-services/language-service/sentiment-opinion-mining/how-to/use-containers#run-the-container-with-docker-run

```
docker run --rm -it -p 5000:5000 --memory 8g --cpus 1 \
mcr.microsoft.com/azure-cognitive-services/textanalytics/
sentiment:{IMAGE_TAG} \
Eula=accept \
Billing={ENDPOINT_URI} \
ApiKey={API_KEY}
```

- {ENDPOINT_URI}

The endpoint for accessing the API. You can find it on your resource's Key and endpoint page, on the Azure portal.

https://<your-custom-subdomain>.cognitiveservices.azure.com

9) A

To create a free Azure resource in the West US Azure region for generating captions of images automatically, you should use the following code:

```
create_resource(client, "res1", "ComputerVision", "F0", "westus")
```

Explanation:

The "ComputerVision" kind is suitable for generating captions of images automatically.

For a free tier resource, the "F0" account tier should be used.

The specified location is "westus," which aligns with the requirement for the West US Azure region.

Therefore, option A is the correct code to use.

There is free tier available for Computer Vision service.

- Free - Web/Container

- 20 per minute

- 5,000 free transactions per month

Reference:

https://learn.microsoft.com/en-us/azure/cognitive-services/cognitive-services-apis-create-account-client-library?pivots=programming-language-csharp#create-a-cognitive-services-resource-c

To create and subscribe to a new Cognitive Services resource, use the Create method. This method adds a new billable resource to the resource group you pass in. When creating your new resource, you'll need to know the "kind" of service you want to use, along with its pricing tier (or SKU) and an Azure location. The following method takes all of these as arguments and creates a resource.

10) D

Regenerates the specified account key for the specified Cognitive Services account.

The new secondary subscription key was created.

It will regenerate the 2nd key.

B is wrong. Query key is for search service. The Rest request of create query key is like POST.

Reference:

https://management.azure.com/subscriptions/

{subscriptionId}/resourceGroups/{resourceGroupName}/
providers/Microsoft.Search/searchServices/
{searchServiceName}/createQueryKey/{name}?api-
version=2021-04-01-preview

https://docs.microsoft.com/en-us/rest/api/
searchmanagement/2021-04-01-preview/query-keys/create

11) ACF

File 2 and 5 are excluded.

New service limits now go up to 500MB so...

File 1, 3, and 6 are correct for "training the model", however if MSFT remove the word "training" from the question - be careful.

Input requirements:

Form Recognizer works on input documents that meet these requirements:

Format must be JPG, PNG, PDF (text or scanned), or TIFF. Text-embedded PDFs are best because there's no possibility of error in character extraction and location.

File size must be less than 50 MB.

Reference:

https://docs.microsoft.com/en-us/azure/cognitive-services/
form-recognizer/overview

https://docs.microsoft.com/en-gb/learn/modules/work-form-
recognizer/3-get-started

https://docs.microsoft.com/en-us/azure/applied-ai-services/
form-recognizer/service-limits?tabs=v21

12) ABF

The correct answers are:

A. The index size will increase.

B. Query times will increase.

F. Azure Key Vault is required.

Explanation:

A. When enabling server-side encryption with customer-managed keys (CMK), the encrypted data typically results in a larger size, so the index size is likely to increase.

B. The process of encrypting and decrypting data with customer-managed keys can introduce additional computational overhead, potentially leading to an increase in query times.

F. Azure Key Vault is required to securely store and manage the customer-managed keys (CMK) used for server-side encryption.

Therefore, the implications of enabling server-side encryption with customer-managed keys (CMK) in Azure Cognitive Search include an increase in index size, potentially longer query times, and the requirement for Azure Key Vault to manage the keys securely.

Use AKV for customer managed key.

Reference:

"Customer-managed keys require an additional billable service, Azure Key Vault, which can be in a different region, but under the same subscription, as Azure Cognitive Search. Enabling

CMK encryption will increase index size and degrade query performance."

Same document also lists Azure Key Vault as a requirement:

https://docs.microsoft.com/en-us/azure/search/search-security-overview#data-protection

13) A

The correct answer is:

A. Transparency

Explanation:

Transparency in AI involves making the processes and decisions of AI systems understandable and accessible to users.

Notifying users that their data has been processed by the sales system aligns with the principle of transparency, as it keeps users informed about how their data is being utilized.

Transparent communication builds trust and helps users understand the implications of data processing, contributing to ethical and responsible AI practices.

Therefore, the action of notifying users about the data processing helps meet the responsible AI principle of transparency.

Reference:

"When an AI application relies on personal data, such as a facial recognition system that takes images of people to recognize them; you should make it clear to the user how their data is used and retained, and who has access to it."

https://docs.microsoft.com/en-us/learn/paths/prepare-for-aiengineering/

14) B

B. No

Explanation: The provided solution is incorrect. Deploying service1 and a public endpoint to a new virtual network and configuring Azure Private Link does not align with the goal of enabling direct connectivity from app1 to service1 without routing traffic over the public internet. Azure Private Link is used for secure access to Azure services over the Azure backbone network, but in this case, deploying a public endpoint contradicts the goal of avoiding public internet routing.

A more suitable approach would be to deploy service1 within the same virtual network as app1 or establish a virtual network peering between vnet1 (where vm1 is located) and the new virtual network containing service1. This way, you can achieve direct connectivity within the Azure environment without relying on the public internet.

You should create a private link with private endpoint.

The Azure Private Link should use a private endpoint, not a public endpoint.

Private Link service can be accessed from approved private endpoints in any public region.

Reference:

https://docs.microsoft.com/en-us/azure/private-link/private-link-overview

15) B

B. No

Explanation: The provided solution does not meet the goal. Deploying service1 with a public endpoint and configuring an IP firewall rule does not ensure that app1 can connect directly to service1 without routing traffic over the public internet. A public endpoint means that the service is accessible over the public internet, and configuring an IP firewall rule might restrict access but does not eliminate the need for public internet routing.

To achieve the goal, you should deploy service1 within the same Azure virtual network as app1 or establish a virtual network peering between vnet1 (where vm1 is located) and the virtual network containing service1. This way, you can enable direct connectivity within the Azure environment without relying on the public internet.

Instead deploy service1 and a private (not public) endpoint to a new virtual network, and you configure Azure Private Link.

Reference:

https://learn.microsoft.com/en-us/azure/search/service-create-private-endpoint#why-use-a-private-endpoint-for-secure-access

Private Endpoints for Azure Cognitive Search allow a client on a virtual network to securely access data in a search index over a Private Link. The private endpoint uses an IP address from the virtual network address space for your search service. Network traffic between the client and the search service traverses over the virtual network and a private link on the Microsoft backbone network, eliminating exposure from the public internet.

16) B

B. No

Explanation:

Deploying service1 with a public endpoint and configuring a network security group (NSG) for vnet1 does not meet the goal of enabling direct connectivity from app1 to service1 without routing traffic over the public internet. Here's why:

Public Endpoint: Deploying service1 with a public endpoint means that it is accessible over the public internet. This is contrary to the goal of avoiding public internet routing.

Network Security Group (NSG) for vnet1: While an NSG can control inbound and outbound traffic within a virtual network, it does not eliminate the need for public internet routing. An NSG focuses on controlling traffic within the virtual network and does not address the direct connectivity requirement without going over the public internet.

To achieve the goal, consider deploying service1 within the same Azure virtual network as app1 or establishing a virtual network peering between vnet1 (where vm1 is located) and the virtual network containing service1. This approach ensures direct connectivity within the Azure environment without relying on the public internet.

Instead deploy service1 and a private (not public) endpoint to a new virtual network, and you configure Azure Private Link.

Reference:

https://learn.microsoft.com/en-us/azure/search/service-create-private-endpoint#why-use-a-private-endpoint-for-secure-access

Private Endpoints for Azure Cognitive Search allow a client on a virtual network to securely access data in a search index over a Private Link. The private endpoint uses an IP address from the virtual network address space for your search service. Network traffic between the client and the search service traverses over the virtual network and a private link on the Microsoft backbone network, eliminating exposure from the public internet.

17) A

The correct answer is:

A. Anomaly Detector

Explanation:

Anomaly Detector: This Azure service is specifically designed to detect unusual patterns or anomalies in time series data. In the context of predictive maintenance and IoT sensor data, Anomaly Detector is well-suited to identify unusual values or patterns that may indicate potential machinery failures.

Cognitive Search, Form Recognizer, and Custom Vision: These services are not designed for time series anomaly detection. Cognitive Search is focused on enhancing search capabilities, Form Recognizer is for extracting information from documents, and Custom Vision is for building custom image classification models.

Therefore, for identifying unusual values in time series data for predictive maintenance, Anomaly Detector is the appropriate

Azure service.

Reference:

https://learn.microsoft.com/en-us/azure/cognitive-services/anomaly-detector/overview

Anomaly Detector is an AI service with a set of APIs, which enables you to monitor and detect anomalies in your time series data with little machine learning (ML) knowledge, either batch validation or real-time inference.

18) 1) b, 2) c

We need to convert Streaming MP3 Data.

So, option 1 is eliminated, as it's not an Audio Streaming function. rest 3 contains the keyword Stream.

But default audio stream format is WAV, and here we are passing MP3, so other than WAV, we need to pass compressed audio format, so correct answer is: AudioStreamFormat.GetCompressedFormat.

and we need to recognize the speech to convert into the text, so, Speech Recognizer.

Reference:

GetCompressedFormat

https://docs.microsoft.com/en-us/dotnet/api/microsoft.cognitiveservices.speech.audio.audiostreamformat.getcompressedformat?view=azure-dotnet

SpeechRecognizer

https://docs.microsoft.com/en-us/dotnet/api/
microsoft.cognitiveservices.speech.speechrecognizer.-ctor?
view=azure-
dotnet#Microsoft_CognitiveServices_Speech_SpeechRecognizer
__ctor_Microsoft_CognitiveServices_Speech_SpeechConfig_Micr
osoft_CognitiveServices_Speech_Audio_AudioConfig_

19) 1) a, 2) a, 3) b

1. Face

2. Face

3. Speech

To address the given requirements for the online training solution, you should use the following Azure Cognitive Services:

1) From a learner's video feed, verify whether the learner is present:

a. Face

2) From learner's facial expression in the video feed, verify whether the learner is paying attention:

a. Face

3) From learner's audio feed, detect whether the learner is talking:

b. Speech

Explanation:

Face API: The Face API can be used to analyze and detect faces in images or video streams. It can determine the presence of faces in a video feed, and it also provides capabilities for analyzing facial expressions, which can be used to infer attention levels.

Speech API: The Speech API is designed for speech recognition and can be used to detect whether a learner is talking by analyzing the audio feed. It provides the ability to transcribe spoken words and identify speakers.

Text Analytics: This service is not directly applicable to the requirements of analyzing video and audio feeds for the presence, attention, or speech of learners. Therefore, Text Analytics is not the suitable choice for this scenario.

Reference:

https://learn.microsoft.com/en-us/azure/cognitive-services/computer-vision/overview-identity#face-detection-and-analysis

Face detection is required as a first step in all the other scenarios. The Detect API detects human faces in an image and returns the rectangle coordinates of their locations. It also returns a unique ID that represents the stored face data. This is used in later operations to identify or verify faces.

Optionally, face detection can extract a set of face-related attributes, such as head pose, age, emotion, facial hair, and glasses. These attributes are general predictions, not actual classifications. Some attributes are useful to ensure that your application is getting high-quality face data when users add themselves to a Face service. For example, your application could advise users to take off their sunglasses if they're wearing sunglasses.

20) DE

D. Azure Cognitive Search

E. Azure App Service

Then these resources are indeed automatically created when provisioning a QnA Maker service in a new resource group (RG1) along with an App Service plan (AP1) within RG1.

Explanation:

Azure Cognitive Search is used by QnA Maker to enable efficient and powerful search capabilities. When you create a QnA Maker service, Azure Cognitive Search is automatically provisioned to support search functionality.

Azure App Service hosts and manages the QnA Maker service. When you provision the QnA Maker service, an Azure App Service is automatically created to host and run the service.

At the creation, we have to precise Azure Search an Azure Web App details.

"When you create a QnAMaker resource, you host the data in your own Azure subscription. Azure Search is used to index your data." & "When you create a QnAMaker resource, you host the runtime in your own Azure subscription. App Service is the compute engine that runs the QnA Maker queries for you."

Reference:

https://docs.microsoft.com/en-us/azure/cognitive-services/qnamaker/how-to/set-up-qnamaker-service-azure?tabs=v1#delete-azure-resources

21) B

The correct answer is:

B. The Access control (IAM) page for the authoring resources in the Azure portal

Explanation:

To add more contributors to a Language Understanding (classic) resource, you would typically use the Access control (IAM) page specifically designed for the authoring resources within the Azure portal. This page allows you to manage and assign roles to individuals or service principals, granting them the necessary permissions to contribute to the language model, such as authoring intents, entities, and other components.

Reference:

https://learn.microsoft.com/en-us/azure/cognitive-services/luis/luis-how-to-collaborate#add-contributor-to-azure-authoring-resource

In the Azure portal, find your Language Understanding (LUIS) authoring resource. It has the type LUIS. Authoring. In the resource's Access Control (IAM) page, add the role of contributor for the user that you want to contribute.

22) A

Yes. Migrating to a higher tier can provide increased resources and capacity, potentially reducing the likelihood of throttling.

Migrating to a higher tier in Azure Cognitive Search can provide more resources, such as increased storage, throughput, and replicas, which can help reduce the likelihood of search query requests being throttled.

A simple fix to most throttling issues is to throw more resources at the search service (typically replicas for query-based throttling, or partitions for indexing-based throttling). However, increasing replicas or partitions adds cost, which is why it is important to know the reason why throttling is occurring at all.

Reference:

https://docs.microsoft.com/en-us/azure/search/search-performance-analysis

https://learn.microsoft.com/en-us/azure/search/search-sku-tier

23) 1) b, 2) d

1) b. Speech to Text

with AutoDetectSourceLanguageConfig. It can't be Text Analytics because the input is callers' voice.

2) d. Text to Speech: the output is voice.

Reference:

https://learn.microsoft.com/en-us/azure/cognitive-services/speech-service/language-identification?tabs=once&pivots=programming-language-csharp#speech-to-text

You use Speech to text recognition when you need to identify the language in an audio source and then transcribe it to text.

https://learn.microsoft.com/en-us/azure/cognitive-services/speech-service/text-to-speech

Text to speech enables your applications, tools, or devices to convert text into humanlike synthesized speech. The text to speech capability is also known as speech synthesis. Use humanlike prebuilt neural voices out of the box, or create a custom neural voice that's unique to your product or brand.

24) C

The correct answer is:

C. Use the FormRecognizerClient client and the StartRecognizeReceiptsFromUri method.

Explanation:

To extract data from receipts using Form Recognizer and the SDK with a prebuilt model, you should use the FormRecognizerClient (not FormTrainingClient) since you are working with an existing prebuilt model.

The method StartRecognizeReceiptsFromUri is specifically designed for extracting information from receipts when using a URI as the source. This method is suitable for scenarios where you have receipts accessible from a URL.

Therefore, option C is the correct choice for extracting data from receipts with a prebuilt model using the Form Recognizer SDK.

private static async Task AnalyzeReceipt(

FormRecognizerClient recognizerClient, string receiptUri)

{

RecognizedFormCollection receipts = await recognizerClient.StartRecognizeReceiptsFromUri(new Uri(receiptUrl)).WaitForCompletionAsync();

Reference:

https://learn.microsoft.com/en-us/dotnet/api/ azure.ai.formrecognizer.formrecognizerclient?view=azure- dotnet

The client to use to connect to the Form Recognizer Azure Cognitive Service to recognize information from forms and images and extract it into structured data. It provides the ability to analyze receipts, business cards, and invoices, to recognize form content, and to extract fields from custom forms with models trained on custom form types.

25) D

Question says: ..."You need to configure an enrichment pipeline to perform optical character recognition (OCR) and "text analytics"... Just because of this second requirement Answer is a Multi Cognitive Service (D), alone vision service (=OCR won't make any text analytics, text extraction is not a text analytics!)

Reference:

https://learn.microsoft.com/en-us/azure/search/cognitive-search-attach-cognitive-services?tabs=portal

When configuring an optional AI enrichment pipeline in Azure Cognitive Search, you can enrich a limited number of documents free of charge. For larger and more frequent workloads, you should attach a billable multi-service Cognitive Services resource.

A multi-service resource references "Cognitive Services" as the offering, rather than individual services, with access granted through a single API key. This key is specified in a skill set and allows Microsoft to charge you for using these APIs:

- Computer Vision for image analysis and optical character recognition (OCR).

- Language service for language detection, entity recognition, sentiment analysis, and key phrase extraction.

- Translator for machine text translation.

26) B

B. No

Explanation: While adding indexes to your Azure Cognitive Search service may improve search performance and efficiency, it may not directly address the issue of query throttling. Throttling can occur due to various factors such as exceeding service limits, resource constraints, or excessive usage.

To specifically address query throttling, you might need to consider other actions such as scaling your service tier to accommodate increased query volume, optimizing queries, or potentially implementing caching strategies. Simply adding indexes, while beneficial for search functionality, may not be sufficient to eliminate query throttling concerns.

"How your search queries perform is directly connected to the size and complexity of your indexes. The smaller and more optimized your indexes, the fast Azure Cognitive Search can respond to queries.

If your index has been optimized but the performance still isn't where it needs to be, you can choose to scale up or scale out your search service.

If you've applied all of the above and still have individual queries that don't perform, you can scale out your index. Depending on the service tier you used to create your search solution, you can add up to 12 partitions. Partitions are the physical storage where your index resides. By default, all new search indexes are created with a single partition. If you add more partitions, the index is stored across them. For example, if your index is 200 GB and you've four partitions, each partition contains 50 GB of your index.

Adding extra partitions can help with performance as the search engine can run in parallel in each partition.

Reference:

https://learn.microsoft.com/en-us/azure/search/search-performance-analysis#throttling-behaviors

27) B

B. No

Explanation: Enabling customer-managed key (CMK) encryption is a security measure and does not directly address the issue of search query throttling. Throttling is typically related to the volume of search queries, resource constraints, or other performance-related factors.

To address search query throttling, you may need to consider actions such as scaling your service tier to accommodate increased query volume, optimizing queries, or implementing caching strategies. Enabling CMK encryption, while important for securing your data, is not a solution to mitigate search query throttling directly.

Reference:

https://learn.microsoft.com/en-us/azure/search/search-performance-analysis#throttling-behaviors

Throttling occurs when the search service is at capacity. Throttling can occur during queries or indexing. From the client side, an API call results in a 503 HTTP response when it has been throttled. During indexing, there's also the possibility of receiving a 207 HTTP response, which indicates that one or more items failed to index. This error is an indicator that the search service is getting close to capacity.

A simple fix to most throttling issues is to throw more resources at the search service (typically replicas for query-based throttling, or partitions for indexing-based throttling). However, increasing replicas or partitions adds cost, which is why it's important to know the reason why throttling is occurring at all. Investigating the conditions that cause throttling will be explained in the next several sections.

28) A

A. Yes

Explanation: Deploying service1 and a private endpoint to vnet1 enables a direct connection between app1 and service1 without routing traffic through the public internet. Private endpoints allow you to access Azure Cognitive Search services over a private connection, ensuring that the traffic remains within the Azure backbone network and doesn't traverse the public internet. This solution aligns with the goal of enabling a secure and direct connection between app1 and service1 within the same virtual network.

A private endpoint is a network interface that uses a private IP address from your virtual network. This network interface connects you privately and securely to a service powered by Azure Private Link. By enabling a private endpoint, you're bringing the service into your virtual network.

The service could be an Azure service such as:

෴ Azure Storage

෴ Azure Cosmos DB

↝ Azure SQL Database

↝ Your own service using a Private Link Service.

Reference:

https://docs.microsoft.com/en-us/azure/private-link/private-endpoint-overview

https://learn.microsoft.com/en-us/azure/search/service-create-private-endpoint#why-use-a-private-endpoint-for-secure-access

Private Endpoints for Azure Cognitive Search allow a client on a virtual network to securely access data in a search index over a Private Link. The private endpoint uses an IP address from the virtual network address space for your search service. Network traffic between the client and the search service traverses over the virtual network and a private link on the Microsoft backbone network, eliminating exposure from the public internet.

29) D

Inclusiveness: AI systems should empower everyone and engage people.

Direct Line Speech is a robust, end-to-end solution for creating a flexible, extensible voice assistant. It is powered by the Bot Framework and its Direct Line

Speech channel, that is optimized for voice-in, voice-out interaction with bots.

Incorrect:

B is wrong: The Active learning suggestions feature allows you to improve the quality of your knowledge base by suggesting alternative questions, based on user- submissions, to your question-and-answer pair. You review those suggestions, either adding them to existing questions or rejecting them.

Direct Line Speech lets the bot speak out loud. This supports Microsoft's goal of AI Inclusiveness because you can include people with disabilities.

Reference:

https://learn.microsoft.com/en-us/azure/cognitive-services/speech-service/direct-line-speech

Direct Line Speech is a robust, end-to-end solution for creating a flexible, extensible voice assistant. It is powered by the Bot Framework and its Direct Line Speech channel, that is optimized for voice-in, voice-out interaction with bots.

Voice assistants listen to users and take an action in response, often speaking back. They use speech to text to transcribe the user's speech, then take action on the natural language understanding of the text. This action frequently includes spoken output from the assistant generated with text to speech.

30) 1) b, 2) b

1) b.

https://eastus.api.cognitive.microsoft.com

2) b.

/text/analytics/v3.1/languages

NOTE:

Pay special attention to the Sample Request provided. Request to the API should be of the form:

POST {Endpoint}/text/analytics/v3.0/languages

Where the {Endpoint} as stated under the sub-heading "URI Parameters" was described as quoted here (see "Description" column of the table):

"Supported Cognitive Services endpoints (protocol and hostname, for example: https://westus.api.cognitive.microsoft.com)."

So the sample given shows the correct format of the *endpoint* as https://{location}.api.cognitive.microsoft.com

31) B

B. a table projection

To analyze the extracted information from the Azure Cognitive Search index with Microsoft Power BI, you should add a table projection to the indexing. This will allow you to present the data in a tabular format that can be easily imported and analyzed by Power BI with minimal development effort.

" Use Power BI for data exploration. This tool works best when the data is in Azure Table Storage. Within Power BI, you can manipulate data into new tables that are easier to query and analyze"

"Table projections are recommended for scenarios that call for data exploration, such as analysis with Power BI or workloads that consume data frames."

See below to understand the workflow:

Purchase Orders (POs) -> Form Recognizer -> OCR -> JSON (extracted info from POs) -> Shaper skill -> JSON -> Table Projection -> JSON -> Power BI

Reference:

Define a table projection https://learn.microsoft.com/en-us/azure/search/knowledge-store-projections-examples#define-a-table-projection

32) A

A. Yes

Explanation: Adding replicas to your Azure Cognitive Search service can increase query capacity and help reduce the likelihood of search query requests being throttled. Replicas provide additional copies of the search index distributed across different nodes, which allows the service to handle a higher volume of queries.

By increasing the number of replicas, you enhance the search service's ability to handle concurrent queries, improving performance and minimizing the chances of throttling. Therefore, adding replicas aligns with the goal of reducing the likelihood of search query requests being throttled.

A simple fix to most throttling issues is to throw more resources at the search service (typically replicas for query-based throttling, or partitions for indexing-based throttling). However, increasing replicas or partitions adds cost, which is why it is important to know the reason why throttling is occurring at all.

Reference:

https://learn.microsoft.com/en-us/azure/search/search-performance-analysis#throttling-behaviors

Throttling occurs when the search service is at capacity. Throttling can occur during queries or indexing. From the client side, an API call results in a 503 HTTP response when it has been throttled. During indexing, there's also the possibility of receiving a 207 HTTP response, which indicates that one or more items failed to index. This error is an indicator that the search service is getting close to capacity.

A simple fix to most throttling issues is to throw more resources at the search service (typically replicas for query-based throttling, or partitions for indexing-based throttling). However, increasing replicas or partitions adds cost, which is why it's important to know the reason why throttling is occurring at all. Investigating the conditions that cause throttling will be explained in the next several sections.

https://learn.microsoft.com/en-us/azure/search/search-performance-tips#index-size-and-schema

However, if the index is right-sized, the only other calibration you can make is to increase capacity: either by adding replicas or upgrading the service tier.

So, adding replicas and upgrading the sku is two valid answers for this question.

Quote "In Cognitive Search, replicas are copies of your index." at https://learn.microsoft.com/en-us/azure/search/search-reliability

33) 1) b, 2) b

1. Create a private endpoint

2. Use Azure roles

https://learn.microsoft.com/en-us/azure/search/service-create-private-endpoint#why-use-a-private-endpoint-for-secure-access

Private Endpoints for Azure Cognitive Search allow a client on a virtual network to securely access data in a search index over a Private Link. The private endpoint uses an IP address from the virtual network address space for your search service. Network traffic between the client and the search service traverses over the virtual network and a private link on the Microsoft backbone network, eliminating exposure from the public internet.

https://learn.microsoft.com/en-us/azure/search/search-security-rbac?tabs=config-svc-portal%2Croles-portal%2Ctest-portal%2Ccustom-role-portal%2Cdisable-keys-portal#grant-access-to-a-single-index

In some scenarios, you may want to limit application's access to a single resource, such as an index.

The portal doesn't currently support role assignments at this level of granularity, but it can be done with PowerShell or the Azure CLI.

34) A

To ensure that the entire dataset is simultaneously scanned for anomalies in sensor data from the past 24 hours, you should employ:

A. Batch

Explanation:

Batch Detection: This method involves analyzing the data in fixed-size intervals or batches. In this scenario, you would process the entire dataset at once, making it suitable for identifying anomalies in a historical context, such as sensor data from the past 24 hours.

Streaming Detection (B): Streaming is typically used for real-time or near-real-time analysis of data as it flows. It might not be the most efficient choice for scanning the entire historical dataset simultaneously.

Change Points (C): Change point detection is focused on identifying points in time where a significant change occurs in the data distribution. While it's related to anomaly detection, it might not directly address the requirement of scanning the entire dataset simultaneously.

Therefore, for this scenario, Batch Detection (Option A) is the appropriate choice to analyze the entire historical dataset for anomalies.

Reference:

https://learn.microsoft.com/en-us/azure/cognitive-services/anomaly-detector/overview#univariate-anomaly-detection

Batch detection

Use your time series to detect any anomalies that might exist throughout your data. This operation generates a model using your entire time series data, with each point analyzed with the same model.

35) Answer:

1) b. Provision an on-premises Kubernetes cluster that is isolated from the internet.

2) c. Pull an image from the Microsoft Container Registry (MCR).

3) d. Run the container and specify an API key and the Endpoint

URL of the Cognitive Services resource.

Explanation:

1. Provision an on-premises Kubernetes cluster that is isolated from the internet (b):

   - Ensure that the on-premises Kubernetes cluster is set up in an isolated environment, enhancing the security of confidential documents.

2. Pull an image from the Microsoft Container Registry (MCR) (c):

   - Retrieve the required container image from a secure and private registry like Microsoft Container Registry (MCR), ensuring the integrity and authenticity of the image.

3. Run the container and specify an API key and the Endpoint URL of the Cognitive Services resource (d):

   - Execute the containerized application while providing the necessary security credentials (API key) and the endpoint URL to access the Azure Cognitive Services resource.

These steps ensure that the application can make requests to the Language service endpoint securely while keeping confidential documents on-premises.

Reference:

1. Provision on-premise k8 cluster that is isolated from Internet

2. Pull image from MCR

3. Run container and specify API key and endpoint URL of Cognitive Services Services

https://learn.microsoft.com/en-us/azure/cognitive-services/containers/disconnected-containers

Containers enable you to run Cognitive Services APIs in your own environment, and are great for your specific security and data governance requirements. Disconnected containers enable you to use several of these APIs disconnected from the internet.

https://learn.microsoft.com/en-us/azure/cognitive-services/ containers/disconnected-container-faq#how-do-i-download-the-disconnected-containers

These containers are hosted on the Microsoft Container Registry and available for download on Microsoft Artifact Registry and Docker Hub. You won't be able to run the container if your Azure subscription has not been approved after completion of the request form.

36)

[1] b. subscriptions/8d3591aa-96b8-4737-ad09-00f9b1ed35ad

[2] b. Microsoft.CognitiveServices

Explanation:

The Subscription ID in the request URL should match the actual Subscription ID from the provided configurations, so [1] should be b. subscriptions/8d3591aa-96b8-4737-ad09-00f9b1ed35ad.

For creating a resource for sentiment analysis and OCR, you would typically use Microsoft.CognitiveServices, so [2] should be b. Microsoft.CognitiveServices.

Therefore, the correct options are [1] b and [2] b.

Reference:

1. subscriptions/8d3591aa-96b8-4737-ad09-00f9b1ed35ad

2. Microsoft.CognitiveServices

https://learn.microsoft.com/en-us/azure/cognitive-services/
cognitive-services-apis-create-account?tabs=multiservice
%2Canomaly-detector%2Clanguage-service%2Ccomputer-
vision%2Cwindows#types-of-cognitive-services-resources

You can access Azure Cognitive Services through two different
resources: A multi-service resource, or a single-service one.

- Multi-service resource:

Access multiple Azure Cognitive Services with a single key and
endpoint.

Consolidates billing from the services you use.

37) A

A. Face

Explanation:

Embed facial recognition into your apps for a seamless and
highly secured user experience. No machine-learning expertise
is required. Features include face detection that perceives facial
features and attributes—such as a face mask, glasses, or face
location—in an image, and identification of a person by a match
to your private repository or via photo ID.

Reference:

https://azure.microsoft.com/en-us/services/cognitive-services/
face/

https://learn.microsoft.com/en-us/azure/cognitive-services/
computer-vision/overview-identity#face-detection-and-

analysis

Face detection is required as a first step in all the other scenarios. The Detect API detects human faces in an image and returns the rectangle coordinates of their locations. It also returns a unique ID that represents the stored face data. This is used in later operations to identify or verify faces.

Optionally, face detection can extract a set of face-related attributes, such as head pose, age, emotion, facial hair, and glasses. These attributes are general predictions, not actual classifications. Some attributes are useful to ensure that your application is getting high-quality face data when users add themselves to a Face service. For example, your application could advise users to take off their sunglasses if they're wearing sunglasses.

38) B

You have an Azure Cognitive Search solution and a collection of blog posts with a category field. To meet specific requirements, including the category field in search results, allowing users to search for words in the category field, and enabling drill-down filtering based on category, you should configure the following index attributes for the category field:

B. searchable, facetable, and retrievable

Explanation:

searchable: Enables users to search for words in the category field.

facetable: Allows users to perform drill-down filtering based on the category.

retrievable: Ensures that the category field is included in the search results.

This configuration aligns with the stated requirements and supports efficient search, filtering, and retrieval operations on the category field within your Azure Cognitive Search solution.

Reference:

https://learn.microsoft.com/en-us/rest/api/searchservice/create-index#-field-definitions-

- retrievable

Indicates whether the field can be returned in a search result.

- searchable

Indicates whether the field is full-text searchable and can be referenced in search queries.

- facetable

Indicates whether to enable the field to be referenced in facet queries.

39) B

B. Billing

The Eula, Billing, and ApiKey options must be specified to run the container; otherwise, the container won't start. For more information, see Billing. The ApiKey value is the Key from the Keys and Endpoints page in the LUIS portal and is also available on the Azure Cognitive Services resource keys page.

https://learn.microsoft.com/en-us/azure/cognitive-services/luis/luis-container-configuration#example-docker-run-commands

https://learn.microsoft.com/en-us/azure/cognitive-services/anomaly-detector/anomaly-detector-container-howto#run-the-container-with-docker-run

The Eula, Billing, and ApiKey options must be specified to run the container; otherwise, the container won't start.

https://learn.microsoft.com/en-us/azure/cognitive-services/anomaly-detector/anomaly-detector-container-howto#billing

The Anomaly Detector containers send billing information to Azure, using an Anomaly Detector resource on your Azure account.

Queries to the container are billed at the pricing tier of the Azure resource that's used for the ApiKey parameter.

Azure Cognitive Services containers aren't licensed to run without being connected to the metering or billing endpoint. You must enable the containers to communicate billing information with the billing endpoint at all times. Cognitive Services containers don't send customer data, such as the image or text that's being analyzed, to Microsoft.

https://learn.microsoft.com/en-us/azure/cognitive-services/anomaly-detector/anomaly-detector-container-howto#billing-arguments

- Billing

The endpoint of the Cognitive Services resource that's used to track billing information.

The value of this option must be set to the endpoint URI of a provisioned Azure resource.

40) BD

B. Configure a custom subdomain.

D. Create a private endpoint.

To authenticate with Speech resource keys, all you need is the key and region. To authenticate with a Microsoft Entra token, the Speech resource must have a custom subdomain and use a private endpoint. The Speech service uses custom subdomains with private endpoints only.

https://learn.microsoft.com/en-us/azure/ai-services/speech-service/role-based-access-control#authentication-with-keys-and-tokens says The Speech service uses custom subdomains with private endpoints only.

41) A

a. Some of the files are password protected.

The possible cause of the issue is that some of the files are password protected. Azure AI Document Intelligence may encounter difficulty processing PDF files that are encrypted with a password. To address this, you may need to ensure that the PDF files are not password protected or decrypt them before processing with the Azure AI Document Intelligence service.

The service cannot process password-protected files, and this can cause the service a processing failure for some of the files. Although file size and number of pages can cause failures, the limit for the S0 tier is 500 MB and 2,000 pages.

The S0 tier is sufficient for the file characteristics mentioned.

References:

https://learn.microsoft.com/en-us/azure/ai-services/document-intelligence/concept-invoice?view=doc-intel-4.0.0&viewFallbackFrom=form-recog-3.0.0

https://learn.microsoft.com/en-us/training/modules/work-form-recognizer/

42) BD

Example code:

```
do
{
results = await client.GetReadResultAsync(Guid.Parse(operationId));
}
while ((results.Status == OperationStatusCodes.Running ||
results.Status == OperationStatusCodes.NotStarted));
```

And looking at what getReadAsync and getReadResultAsync methods return.

getReadResultAsync returns Observable<ReadOperationResult> object which contains as status() method.

getReadAsync doesn't have status method. Answer is B and D.

Reference:

https://docs.microsoft.com/en-us/dotnet/api/system.io.stream.readasync?view=net-6.0

https://github.com/Azure-Samples/cognitive-services-quickstart-code/blob/master/dotnet/ComputerVision/ComputerVisionQuickstart.cs

43) C

c. Azure AI Document Intelligence.

Azure AI Document Intelligence is specifically designed for extracting insights and information from documents. It includes capabilities for OCR (Optical Character Recognition) to extract text from scanned receipts, making it a suitable choice for your scenario. Using Azure AI Document Intelligence minimizes development effort because it provides pre-built models and APIs tailored for document processing tasks. It simplifies the process of extracting information from various types of documents, including receipts.

Azure AI Document Intelligence is designed to work with documents such as receipts, as it offers prebuilt models for extracting information from these kinds of documents.

References:

https://learn.microsoft.com/en-us/azure/ai-services/computer-vision/overview-ocr

https://learn.microsoft.com/en-us/training/modules/work-form-recognizer/

44) A

a. Compact domain.

Only Compact domain is correct. The Azure AI Custom Vision service only exports compact domains, and the models generated by compact domains are optimized for the constraints of real-time classification on mobile devices.

Choosing the "Compact" domain for the Azure AI Custom Vision model is the appropriate option for deploying the application on an edge device without internet connectivity. The Compact domain is designed for scenarios where resources are limited, making it suitable for edge deployments with constrained environments. It provides a balance between accuracy and resource efficiency, making it an ideal choice for offline, edge-based applications such as the one described.

References:

https://learn.microsoft.com/en-us/azure/ai-services/custom-vision-service/select-domain

https://learn.microsoft.com/en-us/azure/ai-services/custom-vision-service/export-your-model

https://learn.microsoft.com/en-us/training/modules/classify-images/

45) D

To configure the app to provide output for users with visual impairments in complete sentences using the Computer Vision API, you should perform the following API call:

D. describeImageInStreamAsync

Explanation:

readInStreamAsync: This method is generally used for reading the content of an image stream but does not specifically provide a description suitable for users with vision impairments.

analyzeImagesByDomainInStreamAsync: This is more domain-specific and may not necessarily provide detailed descriptive sentences, especially for users with vision impairments.

tagImageInStreamAsync: While it provides tags related to

objects in the image, it might not deliver a full, coherent sentence describing the overall content.

describeImageInStreamAsync: This method is specifically designed for generating a human-readable description of the content within an image. It is most suitable for providing comprehensive output for users with vision impairments.

Therefore, the appropriate API call for your scenario is D. describeImageInStreamAsync.

The API call you should perform to provide an output in complete sentences for users who are vision impaired is describeImageInStreamAsync.

The describe feature of the Computer Vision API generates a human-readable sentence to describe the contents of an image. This is particularly useful for accessibility purposes, as it allows visually impaired users to understand what is in an image without needing to see it. The describe feature can also be customized to provide additional details or context, if desired.

46) 1) d, 2) c, 3) b

1. Change domain to General (Compact) domain

2. Retrain model using new domain

3. Export model to desired export format

- In the Domains section, select one of the compact domains. Select Save Changes to save the changes.

- From the top of the page, select Train to retrain using the new domain.

- Go to the Performance tab and select Export.

Reference:

https://learn.microsoft.com/en-us/azure/cognitive-services/
Custom-Vision-Service/export-your-model

the model must be retrained after changing the domain to compact.

47) A

The recommended action to align with Microsoft's responsible AI principles while developing an AI solution using Sentiment Analysis for determining bonuses is:

A. Integrate a human review and approval step before implementing decisions impacting the financial situation of the staff.

Explanation:

Integrating a human review and approval step aligns with responsible AI principles by ensuring that there is human oversight and ethical considerations in decisions that impact individuals, such as financial situations.

This step adds an extra layer of accountability and fairness, allowing for intervention if the AI model produces unexpected or potentially biased outcomes.

While leveraging automation and AI is valuable, incorporating human judgment in critical decision-making processes helps mitigate the risks associated with AI biases and errors.

The other options (B, C, D) do not directly address the responsible AI principles in the context of financial impact and ethical considerations.

48) C

To achieve the objective of allowing access to the Language service resource (ta1) exclusively for resources within the virtual network (vnet1) in your Azure subscription, you should configure:

C. the virtual network settings for ta1

Explanation:

Configuring the virtual network settings for ta1 involves associating ta1 with vnet1 explicitly, ensuring that only resources within vnet1 have the capability to access ta1.

This configuration establishes network-level controls, restricting communication to resources within the specified virtual network.

Options A (network security group for vnet1), B (Azure Firewall for vnet1), and D (Language service container for ta1) are not directly related to configuring access restrictions for a Language service resource within a specific virtual network.

Reference:

https://learn.microsoft.com/en-us/azure/cognitive-services/cognitive-services-virtual-networks?tabs=portal

You can configure Cognitive Services resources to allow access only from specific subnets. The allowed subnets may belong to a VNet in the same subscription, or in a different subscription, including subscriptions belonging to a different Azure Active Directory tenant.

49) C

To achieve the primary goal of generating alerts in case of abnormal values while developing a monitoring system for engine sensor data, you should include:

C. Multivariate Anomaly Detection

Explanation:

Application Insights in Azure Monitor (A): While Application Insights is beneficial for monitoring and diagnosing issues in applications, it may not be the most suitable for analyzing and detecting anomalies in sensor data.

Metric alerts in Azure Monitor (B): Metric alerts are valuable for monitoring individual metrics, but for detecting anomalies across multiple correlated metrics, multivariate anomaly detection is more appropriate.

Multivariate Anomaly Detection (C): This technique is well-suited for analyzing multiple variables simultaneously and identifying anomalies that may not be apparent when considering each variable independently. It is especially relevant when dealing with complex systems like engine sensors.

Univariate Anomaly Detection (D): This approach focuses on detecting anomalies in individual variables. While it has its use cases, it might not capture anomalies that are evident only when considering the relationships between multiple variables.

Therefore, for the specified scenario, Multivariate Anomaly Detection (Option C) is the most appropriate choice.

Reference:

https://learn.microsoft.com/en-us/azure/cognitive-services/anomaly-detector/overview#multivariate-anomaly-detection

The Multivariate Anomaly Detection APIs further enable

developers by easily integrating advanced AI for detecting anomalies from groups of metrics, without the need for machine learning knowledge or labeled data. Dependencies and inter-correlations between up to 300 different signals are now automatically counted as key factors. This new capability helps you to proactively protect your complex systems such as software applications, servers, factory machines, spacecraft, or even your business, from failures.

50) B

For hosting App1 in a location with limited connectivity and minimizing costs while utilizing an Azure Cognitive Services model for anomaly detection in a time series data stream, the recommended option is:

B. Azure Container Instances

Explanation:

Azure Kubernetes Service (AKS) (A): While AKS provides container orchestration, it may involve more infrastructure and management complexity, potentially leading to higher costs. It might not be the most cost-effective solution for a scenario with limited connectivity.

Azure Container Instances (B): ACI allows you to run containers without managing the underlying infrastructure. It is a serverless container service, making it a cost-effective choice for scenarios with sporadic connectivity requirements.

A Kubernetes cluster hosted in an Azure Stack Hub integrated system (C): While an Azure Stack Hub integrated system can provide an on-premises environment, setting up a Kubernetes cluster and managing it might be more complex and may not align with the goal of minimizing costs.

The Docker Engine (D): Docker Engine is a container runtime and is not a standalone solution for hosting containers in a production environment. It lacks the orchestration and management features necessary for the described scenario.

Therefore, for the specified requirements, Azure Container Instances (Option B) is the most suitable and cost-effective choice.

Reference:

https://learn.microsoft.com/en-us/azure/cognitive-services/cognitive-services-container-support

51) A

A. custom product and people names.

Substitution errors are due to the model needing more training on custom product names and people names.

Overlapping speakers defines when there are more deletion errors. People talking in the background are detected when there are more insertion errors.

52) C

To ensure support for noisy environments when developing an application for generating notes through speech, you should recommend:

c. custom speech-to-text

Explanation:

The "custom speech-to-text" model allows you to train a model specifically tailored to handle the characteristics of the target application, including scenarios with background noise. This customization helps improve the accuracy of speech recognition in various environments, making it suitable for your requirements.

The custom speech-to-text model is correct, as you need to adapt the model because a factory floor might have ambient noise, which the model should be trained on.

53) B

b. between 0 and 100

A BLEU score is a number between zero and 100. A score of zero indicates a low-quality translation, where nothing in the translation matches the reference. A score of 100 indicates a perfect translation that is identical to the reference. It is unnecessary to attain a score of 100. A BLEU score between 40 and 60 indicates a high-quality translation.

54) C

To enhance the translation quality for documents uploaded by users in an application that utilizes Azure AI Services Document Translation, you should ask users to include:

c. the source language

Explanation:

Knowing the source language is crucial for accurate translation. This information enables the translation service to properly analyze and translate the content. While other details like a summary, file format, and writing style may be useful for certain scenarios, specifying the source language is fundamental to achieve accurate document translation.

If the language of the content in the source document is known, it is recommended to specify the source language in the request to get a better translation.

55) C

between 40 and 60 indicates a high-quality translation.

References:

https://learn.microsoft.com/en-us/azure/ai-services/translator/custom-translator/key-terms

https://learn.microsoft.com/en-us/training/modules/translate-text-with-translator-service/

56) D

For training a model utilizing Conversational Language Understanding (CLU), the available methods are:

d. standard and advanced only

Explanation:

Standard training methods are commonly used for building language models, and advanced training methods provide additional customization and fine-tuning options. These combined methods offer a comprehensive approach to training CLU models.

Both standard and advanced are from CLU. Deterministic is a method from Language Understanding.

References:

https://learn.microsoft.com/en-us/azure/ai-services/language-service/conversational-language-understanding/how-to/train-model?tabs=language-studio#training-modes

https://learn.microsoft.com/en-us/azure/ai-services/luis/how-to/train-test#change-deterministic-training-settings-using-the-version-settings-api

https://learn.microsoft.com/en-us/training/modules/build-language-understanding-model/

57) D

d. separate workflow projects

Orchestration workflow projects do not support the multilingual option, so you need to create a separate workflow project for each language.

References:

https://learn.microsoft.com/en-us/azure/ai-services/language-service/orchestration-workflow/language-support

https://learn.microsoft.com/en-us/training/modules/build-language-understanding-model/

58) A

a. Add utterances for languages that are performing poorly in the model.

Explanation:

By adding more training data, specifically for languages that are performing poorly, you can improve the model's ability to understand and process those languages more effectively.

This approach focuses on addressing the challenges of individual languages within the same model, potentially leading to better overall performance across all supported languages.

With CLU, there is no need to use multiple projects for a model. For example, you can train a model in English and query it in German.

There is no project language, therefore, adding utterances for languages in the model that are performing poorly is the appropriate solution to increase performance.

References:

https://learn.microsoft.com/en-us/training/modules/build-language-understanding-model/

https://learn.microsoft.com/en-us/azure/ai-services/language-service/conversational-language-understanding/concepts/multiple-languages

59) C

To ensure the successful execution of the API call for configuring a question answering solution, you should:

c. Remove any special characters from the call.

Explanation:

The provided synonyms list contains an extraneous comma at the end of the "alterations" array, which is a syntax error.

Removing any unnecessary special characters, such as the trailing comma in this case, will help ensure a well-formed API call and successful execution.

Special characters are not allowed for synonyms.

Synonyms can be added in any order, and the ordering is not considered in any computational logic.

Synonyms can only be added to a project that has at least one question and answer pair.

60) A

When importing FAQ documents into the Azure AI Language question answering service, the types of data that will be extracted during the process include:

a. formatted text, URLs, and bulleted and numbered lists only

Explanation:

The service is designed to handle formatted text, such as content with URLs and lists, to effectively extract and understand information for question answering.

Images and diagrams are not explicitly mentioned in the options, suggesting that they might not be extracted during the import process.

Currently, the extraction of images within documents that are uploaded to question answering for extraction is unsupported, as images need to be reachable via a public URL.

References:

https://learn.microsoft.com/en-us/azure/ai-services/language-

service/question-answering/reference/document-format-
guidelines

https://learn.microsoft.com/en-us/training/modules/build-
qna-solution-qna-maker/

PRACTICE TEST II

1) DRAG DROP:

You've trained a Custom Vision model to recognize a company's products, utilizing the Retail domain.

Your intention is to deploy the model as an integral part of an application designed for Android phones.

Now, you need to get the model ready for deployment.

Which three actions should you perform in sequence?

To answer, move the appropriate actions from the list of actions to the answer area and arrange them in the correct order.

<u>Actions:</u>

a. Change the model domain.

b. Retain the model.

c. Test the model.

Export the model.

Answer area:

1)..

2)..

3)..

4)..

2) You are tasked with developing an application that utilizes Azure AI Vision to analyze and identify animals in images.

Which type of project should you use?

a. image classification

b. image detection

c. object analysis

d. object classification

e. object detection

3) DRAG DROP:

Within a development environment, you possess a Custom Vision resource named acvdev. Additionally, there is a Custom Vision resource named acvprod in a production environment. In acvdev, you've constructed an object detection model named obj1 within a project named proj1. Your objective is to transfer obj1 from acvdev to acvprod.

Which three actions should you perform in sequence?

To answer, move the appropriate actions from the list of actions to the answer area and arrange them in the correct order.

Select and Place:

<u>**Actions:**</u>

a. Use the Export Project endpoint on acvdev.

b. Use the Get Projects endpoint on acvdev.

c. Use the Import Project endpoint on acvprod.

d. Use the ExportIteration endpoint on acvdev.

e. Use the GetIterations endpoint on acvdev.

f. Use the UpdateProject endpoint on acvprod.

Answer area:

1)...

2)...

3)...

4) DRAG DROP:

You are in the process of creating an application designed to identify defects in components manufactured on a factory production line. These components are unique to your business. To assist in detecting prevalent faults, you aim to leverage the capabilities of the Custom Vision API.

Which three actions should you perform in sequence? To answer, move the appropriate actions from the list of actions to the answer area and arrange them in the correct order.

Select and Place:

Actions:

a. Trainer the classifier model.

b. Upload and tag images.

c. Initialize the training dataset.

d. Train the object detection model.

e. Create a project.

Answer area:

1)...

2)...

3)...

5) HOTSPOT:

You are developing a model for an iOS app that involves classifying images of cats and dogs, determining whether each image features a cat or a dog. The Custom Vision service will be utilized for this purpose.

How should you configure the project in the Custom Vision portal?

To answer, choose the appropriate options in the answer area.

Hot Area:

Answer area:

1) Project Types:

a. Classification

b. Object Detection

2) Classification Types:

a. Multiclass (Single tag per image)

 b. Multilabel (Multiple tags per image)

3) Domains:

a. Audit

b. Food

c. General

d. General (compact)

e. Landmarks

f. Landmarks (compact)

g. Retail

 h. Retail (compact)

6) You are managing an Azure Video Analyzer for Media service to enhance the search functionality for your company's website videos. The goal is to enable video searches based on the individuals present in the content. What actions should you take?

A. Establish a person model and link it to the videos.

B. Generate person objects and submit facial images for each individual.

C. Extend invitations to the complete company staff on Video Indexer.

D. Modify the faces within the videos.

E. Submit names for upload to a language model.

7) You employ the Custom Vision service to construct a classifier.

Following the completion of training, it is necessary to assess the performance of the classifier.

Which two metrics are available for review? Each correct answer presents a complete solution.

A. recall

B. F-score

C. weighted accuracy

D. precision

E. area under the curve (AUC)

8) DRAG DROP:

While crafting the Face API call, you need to identify similar faces from a pre-existing list named "employeefaces" that comprises 60,000 images.

How should you fill in the body of the HTTP request?

To answer, move the appropriate values to the correct targets.

Each value may be used once, more than once, or not at all.

Select and Place:

Values:

a. "faceListId"

b. "LargeFaceListId"

c. "matchFace"

d. "matchPerson"

Answer area:

```
{
"faceId": "18c51a87-3a69-47a8-aedc-a54745f708a1",
[                    ] : "employeefaces",
"maxNumOfCandidatesReturned": 1,
"mode": [                    ]
}
```

9) HOTSPOT:

You're creating a test method to validate the outcomes obtained from an invocation of the Computer Vision API, specifically assessing the presence of company logos in images. The API call yields a collection of brand names referred to as "brands." Here's the provided code segment:

```
for brand in image_analysis.brands:
    if brand_confidence >= 0.75:
        print(f"\nLogo of {brand_name} between {brand.rectangle.x}, {brand.rectangle.y} and
{brand.rectangle.w}, {brand.rectangle.h}")
```

For each of the following statements, choose Yes if the statement is true. Otherwise, choose No.

Hot Area:

Answer area:

Statements:

1) The code will return the name of each detected brand with a confidence equal to or higher than 75 percent.

2) The code will return coordinates for the top-left corner of the rectangle that contains the brand logo of the displayed brands.

3) The code will return coordinates for the bottom-right corner of the rectangle that contains the brand logo of the displayed brands.

10) HOTSPOT:

You are creating an application that incorporates the Face API, and you must upload numerous images to a person group.

To answer, choose the appropriate options [1] and [2] in the answer area.

Hot Area:

Answer area:

```
Parallel.For(0, PersonCount, async i =>
{
    Guid personId = persons[i].PersonId;
    string personImageDir = $"/path/to/person/{i}/images";
    foreach (string imagePath in Directory.GetFiles(personImageDir, "*.jpg"))
    {
        using ( [1]  t = File.OpenRead(imagePath))
        {
            await faceClient.PersonGroupPerson. [2]



(personGroupId, personId, t);
        }
    }
});
```

[1] a. File

    b. Stream

    c. Uri

    d. Url

[2] a. AddFaceFromStreamAsync

    b. AddFaceFromUrlAsync

    c. CreateAsync

    d. GetAsync

11) You are developing an application that will utilize Azure AI Vision to analyze and categorize images, creating an image library specifically for animals.

You need to set up the classification type for the Azure AI Vision project. The solution must guarantee that the chosen images exclusively feature a single animal.

Which type of classification should you use?

a. multiclass

b. multilabel

c. singleclass

d. singlelabel

e. unilabel

12) You possess the following Python function to programmatically create Azure Cognitive Services resources:

```
def create_resource(resource_name, kind, account_tier, location):
    parameters = CognitiveServicesAccount(sku=Sku(name=account_tier), kind=kind, location=location, properties={})
    result = client.accounts.create(resource_group_name, resource_name, parameters)
```

Now, you must invoke the function to generate a free Azure resource in the West US Azure region. This resource will be employed for the automatic generation of image captions.

Which code should you use?

A. create_resource("res1", "ComputerVision", "F0", "westus")

B. create_resource("res1", "CustomVision.Prediction", "F0", "westus")

C. create_resource("res1", "ComputerVision", "S0", "westus")

D. create_resource("res1", "CustomVision.Prediction", "S0",

"westus")

13) This question is one in a series that describes a specific scenario. Each question in the series provides a distinct solution that could potentially fulfill the given objectives. Some sets of questions may have multiple correct solutions, while others might not have any correct solutions.

You are creating an application to recognize flower species by training a Custom Vision model. New images of different flower species are provided, and your task is to incorporate these new images into the classifier.

Solution: You add the new images, and then use the Smart Labeler tool.

Does this meet the goal?

A. Yes

B. No

14) HOTSPOT:

You are creating an application that allows users to upload images, and it should satisfy the following criteria:

- Automatically propose alt text for the images.
- Identify inappropriate images and prevent their display.
- Minimize the amount of development work required.

You need to suggest a computer vision endpoint for each requirement.

What should you recommend?

To answer, choose the appropriate options in the answer area.

Hot area:

Answer area:

1) Generate alt text:

a.   https://westus.api.cognitive.microsoft.com/contentmoderator/moderate/v1.0/ProcessImage/Evaluate

b.   https://westus.api.cognitive.microsoft.com/customvision/v3.1/prediction/projectld/classify/iterations/publishedName/image

c.   https://westus.api.cognitive.microsoft.com/vision/v3.2/analyze/?visual Features Adult, Description

2) Detect inappropriate content:

a.   https://westus.api.cognitive.microsoft.com/contentmoderator/moderate/v1.0/ProcessImage/Evaluate

b.   https://westus.api.cognitive.microsoft.com/customvision/v3.1/prediction/projectld/classify/iterations/publishedName/image

c.   https://westus.api.cognitive.microsoft.com/vision/v3.2/analyze/?visual Features Adult, Description

d.   https://westus.api.cognitive.microsoft.com/vision/v3.2/describe?maxCandidates=1

15) You are tasked with developing a solution that employs optical character recognition (OCR) to analyze sensitive documents through the Computer Vision API, with the stipulation that the solution should not be implemented on the public cloud. What actions should you take?

A. Build an on-premises web app to query the Computer Vision endpoint.

B. Host the Computer Vision endpoint in a container on an on-premises server.

C. Host an exported Open Neural Network Exchange (ONNX) model on an on-premises server.

D. Build an Azure web app to query the Computer Vision endpoint.

16) You possess an Azure Cognitive Search solution and a set of handwritten letters stored as JPEG files.

You plan to index the collection. The solution must ensure that queries can be performed on the contents of the letters.

To achieve this, you need to establish an indexer incorporating a skillset.

Which skill should you include?

A. image analysis

B. optical character recognition (OCR)

C. key phrase extraction

D. document extraction

17) HOTSPOT:

You have a vast collection of images in a library, and your task is to categorize the images into three groups: photographs, drawings, or clipart.

Which service endpoint and response property should you use?

To answer, choose the appropriate options in the answer area.

Answer area:

1) Service endpoint:

a. Computer Vision analyze images

b. Computer Vision object detection

c. Custom Vision Image classification

 d. Custom Vision object detection

2) Property:

a. Categories

b. Description

c. imageType

d. metadata

e. objects

18) You possess an application that records live video footage of exam candidates, and your objective is to employ the Face service for the purpose of confirming the authenticity of the individuals appearing in the videos.

What should you do?

A. Call the face detection API and retrieve the face rectangle by using the FaceRectangle attribute.

B. Call the face detection API repeatedly and check for changes to the FaceAttributes.HeadPose attribute.

C. Call the face detection API and use the FaceLandmarks attribute to calculate the distance between pupils.

D. Call the face detection API repeatedly and check for changes to the FaceAttributes.Accessories attribute.

19) You are developing an application that utilizes the Azure AI Video Indexer API to analyze Microsoft Teams meeting recordings. The purpose of the app is to identify images and references related to competing companies.

Which content model should you use?

a. custom brands

b. custom Language

c. custom slate

20) Within your Azure subscription, there exists an AI enrichment pipeline in Azure Cognitive Search, coupled with an Azure Storage account housing 10 GB of scanned documents and images.

Your objective is to index these documents and images, with an emphasis on minimizing the time required for index construction.

What should you do?

A. From the Azure portal, configure parallel indexing.

B. From the Azure portal, configure scheduled indexing.

C. Configure field mappings by using the REST API.

D. Create a text-based indexer by using the REST API.

21) DRAG DROP:

You are required to conduct an analysis of video content to

detect any references to specific company names.

Which three actions should you perform in sequence?

To answer, move the appropriate actions from the list of actions to the answer area and arrange them in the correct order.

Actions:

a. Add the specific company names to the exclude list.

b. Add the specific company names to the include list.

c. From Content model customization, select Language.

d. Sign in to the Custom Vision website.

e. Sign in to the Azure Video Analyzer for Media website.

f. From Content model customization, select Brands.

Answer area:

1)...

2)...

3)...

22) You possess a mobile app designed for handling printed forms, and you require the app to directly transmit images of the forms-to-Forms Recognizer for extracting pertinent information.

To comply with regulations, it is imperative that the image files are not stored in the cloud.

In which format should you send the images to the Form Recognizer API endpoint?

A. raw image binary

B. form URL encoded

C. JSON

23) You are preparing to develop an application that will produce a set of tags for uploaded images, and the application must adhere to the following criteria:

• **Generate tags in the user's selected language.**

• **Support English, French, and Spanish.**

• **Minimize the amount of development work required.**

To meet these requirements, you need to create a function responsible for generating the tags in the preferred language for the application.

Which Azure service endpoint should you use?

A. Content Moderator Image Moderation.

B. Custom Vision image classification.

C. Computer Vision Image Analysis.

D. Custom Translator.

24) This question is one in a series that describes a specific scenario. Each question in the series provides a distinct solution that could potentially fulfill the given objectives. Some sets of questions may have multiple correct solutions, while others might not have any correct solutions.

You are creating an application to recognize flower species by training a Custom Vision model. New images of different

flower species are provided, and your task is to incorporate these new images into the classifier.

Solution: You create a new model, and then upload the new images and labels.

Does this meet the goal?

A. Yes

B. No

25) DRAG DROP:

You operate a factory that manufactures cardboard packaging for food products, and the factory experiences occasional internet connectivity interruptions.

Your packaging requirements dictate that each package must include four samples of every product.

To achieve this, you must develop a Custom Vision model capable of detecting defects in packaging and indicating the defect locations to an operator, while ensuring the presence of four products in each package.

Which project type and domain should you use?

To answer, drag the appropriate options to the correct targets.

Each option may be used once, more than once, or not at all.

Options:

a. Food

b. General

c. General (compact)

d. Image classification

e. Logo

f. Object detection

Answer area:

1) Project type:

2) Domain:

26) HOTSPOT:

You are building a model to detect objects in images.

The performance of the model based on training data is shown in the following exhibit.

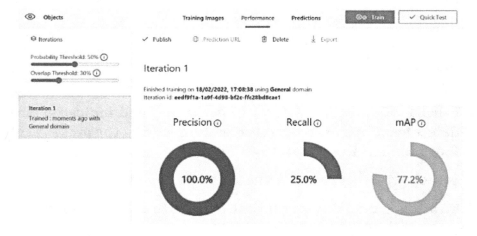

Choose the answer choice that completes each statement based on the information presented in the graphic.

Answer area:

1) The percentage of false positives is [**answer choice**].

a. 0

b. 25

c. 30

d. 50

e. 100

2) The value for the number of true positives divided by the total number of true positives and false negatives is [answer choice] %.

 a. 0

b. 25

c. 30

d. 50

e. 100

27) You are developing an application that will incorporate one million scanned magazine articles, each stored as an image file. To enable the extraction of text from these images, the solution must be designed to minimize development effort.

What should you include in the solution?

A. Computer Vision Image Analysis.

B. The Read API in Computer Vision.

C. Form Recognizer.

D. Azure Cognitive Service for Language.

28) You possess a video file named File1.avi with a size of 20 GB, stored locally. Your goal is to index File1.avi using the Azure Video Indexer website. What is the initial step you should take?

A. Transmit File1.avi to an Azure Storage queue.

B. Transmit File1.avi to the Azure Video Indexer website.

C. Transmit File1.avi to Microsoft OneDrive.

D. Transmit File1.avi to the www.youtube.com webpage.

29) This question is part of a series that describes a specific scenario. Each question in the series presents a distinct solution that could potentially fulfill the given objectives. Some sets of questions may have multiple correct solutions, while others might not have any correct solutions.

You are creating a language model using a Language Understanding service, specifically for searching information on a contact list using an intent called FindContact. A conversational expert provides you with the following set of phrases for training:

- **Find contacts in London.**
- **Who do I know in Seattle?**
- **Search for contacts in Ukraine.**

Your task is to implement the phrase list in Language Understanding.

Solution: You create a new pattern in the FindContact intent.

Does this meet the goal?

A. Yes

B. No

30) This question is one in a series that describes a specific scenario. Each question in the series provides a distinct

solution that could potentially fulfill the given objectives. Some sets of questions may have multiple correct solutions, while others might not have any correct solutions.

You are creating an application to recognize flower species by training a Custom Vision model. New images of different flower species are provided, and your task is to incorporate these new images into the classifier.

Solution: You add the new images and labels to the existing model. You retrain the model, and then publish the model.

Does this meet the goal?

A. Yes

B. No

31) HOTSPOT:

You are building a service to capture lectures delivered in English (United Kingdom). Within this service, there's a method called AppendToTranscriptFile, which accepts translated text and a language identifier.

Your objective is to create code that delivers lecture transcripts to attendees in their respective language, supporting English, French, Spanish, and German.

How should you complete the code? To answer, choose the appropriate options [1] and [2] in the answer area.

Hot Area:

Answer area:

```
static async Task TranslateSpeechAsync()
{
    var config =SpeechTranslationConfig.FromSubscription("69cad5cc-0ab3-4704-bdff-efbf4aa07d85", "uksouth");

    var lang = new List<string> [1]
```

```
config.SpeechRecognitionLanguage = "en-GB";
lang.ForEach(config.AddTargetLanguage);

using var audioConfig = AudioConfig.FromDefaultMicrophoneInput();
using var recognizer = new      [2]            (config, audioConfig);

var result = awit recognizer.RecognizeOnceAsync();
if (result.Reason == ResultReason.TranslatedSpeech)
```

[1]

a. {"en-GB"}

b. {"fr", "de", "es"}

c. {"French", "Spanish", "German"}

d. {languages}

[2]

a. IntentRecognizer

b. SpeakerRecognizer

c. SpeechSynthesizer

d. TranslationRecognizer

32) DRAG DROP:

You're responsible for training a Custom Vision model utilized in a mobile app. You've been provided with 1,000 new images lacking any associated data.

Which three actions should you perform in the Custom Vision portal?

To answer, move the appropriate actions from the list of actions to the answer area and arrange them in the correct order.

Select and Place:

Actions:

a. Upload the images by category.

b. Get suggested tags.

c. Upload all the images.

d. Group the images locally into category folders.

e. Review the suggestions and confirm the tags.

f. Tag the images manually.

Answer area:

1)..

2)..

3)..

33) You're developing a Conversational Language Understanding model for an e-commerce chatbot, where users can provide their billing address through speech or text when prompted by the chatbot. Your task is to create an entity that can effectively capture billing addresses.

Which entity type should you use?

A. machine learned

B. Regex

C. list

D. Pattern.any

34) You are in the process of constructing an Azure WebJob tasked with generating knowledge bases from an array of

URLs. To achieve this, you create a QnAMakerClient object containing the necessary API keys and assign it to a variable named "client." Your next step involves developing a method to initiate the creation of these knowledge bases.

Which two actions should you include in the method?

Each correct answer presents part of the solution.

A. Create a list of FileDTO objects that represents data from the WebJob.

B. Call the client.Knowledgebase.CreateAsync method.

C. Create a list of QnADTO objects that represents data from the WebJob.

D. Create a CreateKbDTO object.

35) HOTSPOT:

You're working on an application incorporating language translation. The application will translate text obtained through a function called getTextToBeTranslated. The text may originate from various languages, and it is crucial that the content stays within the Azure geography of the Americas.

You need to develop code to translate the text to a single language.

How should you complete the code?

To answer, choose the appropriate options [1] and [2] in the answer area.

Hot Area:

```
. . .
var endpoint =    [1]                                              ;
var apiKey = "FF956C68B83B21B38691ABD200A4C606";
var text = getTextToBeTranslated();
var body = '[{"Text":"' + text + '"}]';
var client = new HttpClient();
client.DefaultRequestHeaders.Add("Ocp-Apim-Subscription-Key", apiKey);
  [2]
HttpResponseMessage response;
var content = new StringContent(body, Encoding.UTF8, "application/json");
var response = await client.PutAsync(uri, content);
. . .
```

[1]

a. "https://api.cognitive.microsofttranslator.com/translate"

b. "https://api.cognitive.microsofttranslator.com/transliterate"

c.

"https://api-apc.cognitive.microsofttranslator.com/detect"

d. "https://api-nam.cognitive.microsofttranslator.com/detect"

e. https://api-nam.cognitive.microsofttranslator.com/translate

[2]

a. var uri= endpoint +"?from=en";

b. var uri = endpoint + "?suggestedFrom=en";

c. var uri= endpoint +"?to=en";

36) You are constructing a conversational language understanding model and want to implement active learning.

How can you achieve this?

A. Include show-all-intents=true in the prediction endpoint

query.

B. Activate speech priming.

C. Integrate log=true into the prediction endpoint query.

D. Implement sentiment analysis.

37) HOTSPOT:

You run the following command.
```
docker run --rm -it -p 5000:5000 --memory 10g --cpus 2 \
mcr.microsoft.com/azure-cognitive-services/textanalytics/sentiment\
Eula=accept \
Billing={ENDPOINT_URI} \
ApiKey={API_KEY}
```

For each of the following statements, choose Yes if the statement is true. Otherwise, choose No.

Hot Area:

Answer area:

Statements:

1) Going to http://localhost:5000/status will query the Azure endpoint to verify whether the API key used to start the container is valid.

2) The container logging provider will write log data.

3) Going to http://localhost:5000/swagger will provide the details to access the documentation for the available endpoints.

38) When building a Language Understanding model for an e-commerce platform. You need to construct an entity to capture billing addresses.

What type of entity should you create to capture billing address?

A. machine learned

B. Regex

C. geographyV2

D. Pattern.any

E. list

39) You're in the process of developing a method for an application utilizing the Translator API. The objective is to translate the content of a webpage into Greek (el) while also obtaining a transliteration in the Roman alphabet. To achieve this, you need to construct the URI for the call to the Translator API, starting with the base URI: https://api.cognitive.microsofttranslator.com/translate?api-version=3.0

Which three additional query parameters should you include in the URI?

Each correct answer presents part of the solution.

A. toScript=Cyrl

B. from=el

C. textType=html

D. to=el

E. textType=plain

F. toScript=Latn

40) You need to conduct remote debugging on the endpoint of a chatbot created with the Microsoft Bot Framework.

Which two tools should you install on a local computer?

Each correct answer presents part of the solution.

A. Fiddler

B. Bot Framework Composer

C. Bot Framework Emulator

D. Bot Framework CLI

E. ngrok

F. nginx

41) DRAG DROP:

You are developing a retail chatbot that will utilize a QnA Maker service.

You add a support document internally to train the model, which includes the question: "What is your warranty period?"

Users report that the chatbot returns the default QnA Maker answer when they ask the following question: "How long is the warranty coverage?"

The chatbot returns the accurate response when users inquire with the question: "What is your warranty period?"

Both questions should return the same answer.

You need to increase the accuracy of the chatbot responses.

Which three actions should you perform in sequence?

To answer, move the appropriate actions from the list of actions to the answer area and arrange them in the correct order.

Select and Place:

Actions:

a. Add a new question and answer (QnA) pair.

b. Retrain the model.

c. Add additional questions to the document.

d. Republish the model.

e. Add alternative phrasing to the question and answer (QnA) pair.

Answer area:

1)...

2)...

3)...

42) This question is one of several scenarios presented in a series. Each scenario within the series proposes a distinct solution that could potentially fulfill the stated objectives. Some scenarios might have multiple correct solutions, while others may not have any correct solutions.

You are tasked with constructing a language model through a Language Understanding service. This model is designed for searching information on a contact list specifically for an intent labeled FindContact. To accomplish this, a conversational expert supplies you with a set of phrases for training:

Find contacts in London.

Who do I know in Seattle?

Search for contacts in Ukraine.

Your objective is to implement this phrase list within

Language Understanding.

Solution: You create a new intent for location.

Does this meet the goal?

A. Yes

B. No

43) You are working on training a Language Understanding model for a user support system.

You establish the initial intent, named GetContactDetails, and include 200 examples.

You need to decrease the likelihood of a false positive.

What should you do?

A. Enable active learning.

B. Add a machine learned entity.

C. Add additional examples to the GetContactDetails intent.

D. Add examples to the None intent.

44) DRAG DROP:

You are creating a Language Understanding model for buying tickets, and you have the following utterance for an intent called PurchaseAndSendTickets:

Purchase [2 audit business] tickets to Paris [next Monday] and send tickets to [email@domain.com]

You must choose the entity types.

The approach should leverage built-in entity types to

minimize the requirement for extensive training data whenever it is feasible.

Which entity type should you use for each label?

To answer, drag the appropriate entity types to the correct labels. Each entity type may be used once, more than once, or not at all.

Select and Place:

Entity Types:

a. Email

b. List

c. Regex

d. GeographyV2

e. Machine learned

Answer area:

1) Paris: ....

2) email@domain.com: ....

3) 2 audit business: ....

45) You are developing a bot using Azure AI Bot Service and the Microsoft Bot Framework SDK. You need to design a dialog that prompts users for information in a predefined order.

Which type of dialog should you use?

a. action

b. AskUser

c. question

d. waterfall

46) You construct a Conversational Language Understanding model using the Language Services portal. Subsequently, you export the model in JSON format, as illustrated in the provided sample.

```
{
  "text": "average amount of rain by month at chicago last year",
  "intent": "Weather.CheckWeatherValue",
  "entities": [
    {
      "entity": "Weather.WeatherRange",
      "startPos": 0,
      "endPos": 6,
      "children": []
    },
    {
      "entity": "Weather.WeatherCondition",
      "startPos": 18,
      "endPos": 21,
      "children": []
    },
    {
      "entity": "Weather.Historic",
      "startPos": 23,
      "endPos": 30,
      "children": []
    }
  ]
}
```

To what does the Weather.Historic entity correspond in the utterance?

A. by month

B. chicago

C. rain

D. location

47) You are reviewing the output of Text Analytics for an

application. The analyzed text is: "Our tour guide took us up the Space Needle during our trip to Seattle last week." The output includes the information presented in the following table.

Text	Category	ConfidenceScore
Tour guide	PersonType	0.45
Space Needle	Location	0.38
Trip	Event	0.78
Seattle	Location	0.78
Last week	DateTime	0.80

Which Text Analytics API is used to analyze the text?

A. Entity Linking

B. Named Entity Recognition

C. Sentiment Analysis

D. Key Phrase Extraction

48) You possess an application called App1 designed to analyze social media mentions and ascertain the sentiment of comments, distinguishing between positive and negative expressions.

While conducting tests, you observe that App1 produces negative sentiment analysis results for customer feedback that actually includes positive sentiments.

You must guarantee that App1 incorporates more detailed information in the course of its analysis.

What should you add to the API requests?

a. loggingOptOut=true

b. StringIndexType=TextElements_v8

c. opinionMining=true

49) You are developing an application designed to analyze resumes and redact personal information such as names and addresses. Your task involves configuring the Azure AI Language Personally Identifiable Information (PII) detection feature for the application.

Which categories should you specify in the request?

a. Person, Address, and IP

b. Person and Address only

c. Person, PersonType, and Address

50) You are developing an application that will identify documents containing the names of staff members, utilizing the Azure AI Language Personally Identifiable Information (PII) detection feature. Your task involves configuring the PII detection feature for the application.

Which category should you use?

a. Age

b. DateTime

c. Person

d. PhoneNumber

51) You are building a bot.

You generate a set of questions that a user needs to respond to

in order to navigate through a procedure.

The user has the option to choose a completely different action or inquire about a topic that may not be related to the current subject.

How should you handle this situation in the bot?

a. Disregard everything that the user answered previously, reset the dialog stack, and start from the beginning.

b. Insist that the users complete the current queries first before moving on to the next question.

c. The best solution will depend on the specific case you must solve.

52) You are developing a new bot to facilitate the automated purchase of socks.

How should the bot initiate the conversation?

a. Hello, I'm the bot responsible for your sock orders.

b. Hello sir, I hope you are having a good day.

c. Hey, how can I help you?

53) You are creating a bot using Azure AI Bot Service and the Microsoft Bot Framework Composer.

You need to create a dialog that solicits information from a user and retains the responses throughout the session.

The solution must ensure that collected information is deleted automatically at the end of the session.

Which scope should you use?

a. dialog

b. conversation

c. setting

d. user

54) You are developing a bot with Azure AI Bot Service and the Microsoft Bot Framework Composer.

You need to determine the user's location when they establish a connection with the bot.

Which prebuilt property should you query?

a. turn.activity.locale

b. turn.activity.message.locale

c. turn.conversation.locale

d. turn.message.locale

55) You are developing a bot and wish to perform interactive debugging using the Bot Framework Emulator.

What should you add to the code?

a. a mock dialog

b. a test dialog

c. a trace activity

56) You are developing a bot utilizing Azure AI Bot Service and the Microsoft Bot Framework SDK. The bot will serve both

your organization and partner companies.

You need to configure security for the bot.

What should you use?

a. a multi-tenant app

b. a single-tenant app

c. a user-assigned managed identity

57) You are developing a bot utilizing Azure AI Bot Service and the Microsoft Bot Framework SDK.

You deploy the bot to Azure and set up the bot to utilize the URL: https://chatbot.azurewebsites.net.

You are required to test and debug the bot utilizing the Bot Framework Emulator.

Which URL should you use?

a. http://chatbot.azurewebsites.net/api

b. https://chatbot.azurewebsites.net/api/messages

c. http://chatbot.azurewebsites.net/messages

d. https://chatbot.azurewebsites.net/messages/api

58) You are developing a digital assistant bot to manage new sales requests for your sales department.

When designing the bot, what should you include in the conversational user experience (CUX) guide?

a. a set of CSS rules

b. licensing best practices

c. practical development tips

59) You are developing an application called App1 that utilizes the Image Analysis API.

You are assessing the image analysis process through the following request.

https://*.cognitiveservices.azure.com/computervision/ imageanalysis:analyze? features=read,description

Which results will the request return?

a description of the image content only

b. the visible text in the image and a description of the image content

c. which objects there are in the image and their approximate location

60) You are developing an application that utilizes Azure AI Vision to identify whether people are present in a video feed.

Which Azure AI Vision feature should you use?

a. face detection

b. Image Analysis

c. optical character recognition (OCR)

d. Spatial Analysis

ANSWERS AND EXPLANATION

1) 1) a, 2) b, 2) c, 3) d

a. Change the model domain.

b. Retain the model.

c. Test the model.

d. Export the model.

Explanation:

Change the model domain (a): If you initially trained the model using the Retail domain but need to optimize it for the specific requirements of the Android app, you might consider changing the domain or fine-tuning the model to improve its performance.

Retain the model (b): Ensure that you keep the trained model as it is an essential step before exporting it for deployment. Retaining the model preserves the training and adjustments made during the training phase.

Test the model (c): Before deploying the model to the Android app, it's crucial to conduct thorough testing to ensure that it performs accurately and meets the desired recognition criteria for the company's products.

Export the model (d): Once you've validated that the model

performs well and suits the Android app's requirements, export the model. This step prepares the model for integration into the application for deployment on Android phones.

Reference:

https://docs.microsoft.com/en-us/azure/cognitive-services/ custom-vision-service/export-your-model

2) E

e. object detection.

Object detection returns the coordinates in an image where the applied label(s) can be found, while image classification applies one or more labels to an entire image.

References:

https://learn.microsoft.com/en-us/azure/ai-services/custom-vision-service/overview

https://learn.microsoft.com/en-us/training/modules/detect-objects-images/

3) 1) b, 2) a, 3) c

b. Use the Get Projects endpoint on acvdev: This step involves retrieving information about the projects available in the development environment (acvdev), which includes the project proj1.

a. Use the Export Project endpoint on acvdev: After identifying the project using the Get Projects endpoint, proceed to export the identified project (proj1) from the development environment (acvdev).

c. Use the Import Project endpoint on acvprod: With the exported project file, import it into the production environment (acvprod) using the Import Project endpoint.

This sequence ensures a smooth transition of the object detection model (obj1) from the development to the production environment.

References:

1. Use GetProjects endpoint on acvDEV

2. Use ExportProjects endpoint on acvDEV

3. Use ImportProjects endpoint on avcPROD

https://learn.microsoft.com/en-us/azure/cognitive-services/custom-vision-service/copy-move-projects#get-the-project-id

First call GetProjects to see a list of your existing Custom Vision projects and their IDs. Use the training key and endpoint of your source account.

https://learn.microsoft.com/en-us/azure/cognitive-services/custom-vision-service/copy-move-projects#export-the-project

Call ExportProject using the project ID and your source training key and endpoint.

https://learn.microsoft.com/en-us/azure/cognitive-services/custom-vision-service/copy-move-projects#import-the-project

Call ImportProject using your target training key and endpoint, along with the reference token. You can also give your project a name in its new account.

https://learn.microsoft.com/en-us/azure/cognitive-services/

custom-vision-service/copy-move-projects#process-overview

The process for copying a project consists of the following steps:

- First, you get the ID of the project in your source account you want to copy.

- Then you call the ExportProject API using the project ID and the training key of your source account. You'll get a temporary token string.

- Then you call the ImportProject API using the token string and the training key of your target account. The project will then be listed under your target account.

4) 1) e, 2) b, 3) a

Step 1: Create a project

Create a new project.

Step 2: Upload and tag the images.

Choose training images. Then upload and tag the images.

Step 3: Train the classifier model.

Train the classifier

e. Create a project: Begin by creating a project in the Custom Vision service. This project serves as the foundation for organizing and managing your custom vision tasks.

b. Upload and tag images: After creating the project, proceed to upload relevant images of the components and tag them appropriately. Tagging is essential for associating specific characteristics or faults with the images.

a. Train the classifier model: Following the upload and tagging of images, move on to training the classifier model. This step involves teaching the model to recognize and classify specific faults in the components.

Reference:

https://docs.microsoft.com/en-us/azure/cognitive-services/custom-vision-service/getting-started-build-a-classifier

https://learn.microsoft.com/en-us/azure/cognitive-services/custom-vision-service/quickstarts/image-classification?tabs=visual-studio&pivots=programming-language-csharp

For Type of model

https://azure.microsoft.com/en-us/use-cases/defect-detection-with-image-analysis/

5) 1) a, 2) a, 3) d

Project Types:

Classification (a): In this scenario, you are tasked with determining whether an image contains a cat or a dog. Classification is the suitable project type for this purpose, as it involves assigning each image to a specific category.

Incorrect Answers:

An object detection project is for detecting which objects, if any, from a set of candidates are present in an image.

Classification Types:

Multiclass (Single tag per image) (a): Since each image is expected to contain either a cat or a dog, using a single tag per image (multiclass) is appropriate. This means that each image will be assigned a single label indicating whether it belongs to the "cat" category or the "dog" category.

A multiclass classification project is for classifying images into a set of tags, or target labels. An image can be assigned to one tag only.

Incorrect Answers:

A multilabel classification project is similar, but each image can have multiple tags assigned to it.

Domains:

General (compact) (d):

In the context of an iOS app where resource efficiency is often a consideration, and assuming that the accuracy of the model is acceptable, "General (compact)" would be a suitable choice. This is because the "General (compact)" domain provides a more lightweight model, which aligns well with the constraints of mobile devices.

Reference:

https://learn.microsoft.com/en-us/azure/ai-services/custom-vision-service/export-your-model

https://learn.microsoft.com/en-us/azure/cognitive-services/custom-vision-service/getting-started-build-a-classifier

6) A

Azure Video Analyzer for Media (Video Indexer) supports multiple Person models per account. Once a model is created, you can use it by providing the model ID of a specific Person model when uploading/indexing or reindexing a video. Training a new face for a video updates the specific custom model that the video was associated with.

Note: Azure Video Analyzer for Media (Video Indexer) supports face detection and celebrity recognition for video content. The celebrity recognition feature covers about one million faces based on commonly requested data source such as IMDB, Wikipedia, and top LinkedIn influencers. Faces that aren't recognized by the celebrity recognition feature are detected but left unnamed. Once you label a face with a name, the face and name get added to your account's Person model. Video Indexer will then recognize this face in your future videos and past videos.

Reference:

https://docs.microsoft.com/en-us/azure/media-services/video-indexer/customize-person-model-with-api

https://learn.microsoft.com/en-us/azure/azure-video-indexer/customize-person-model-overview

7) AD

A. recall

D. precision

Explanation:

Recall (A):

Recall, also known as sensitivity or true positive rate, measures the ability of the classifier to correctly identify all relevant instances. It is calculated as the ratio of true positives to the sum of true positives and false negatives.

Precision (D):

Precision assesses the accuracy of positive predictions made by the classifier. It is calculated as the ratio of true positives to the sum of true positives and false positives.

While F-score, weighted accuracy, and area under the curve (AUC) are commonly used metrics, the two metrics specifically mentioned in your options for assessing classifier performance are recall and precision. Therefore, options A (recall) and D (precision) are the correct answers for this scenario.

References:

https://learn.microsoft.com/en-us/azure/cognitive-services/custom-vision-service/getting-started-build-a-classifier#evaluate-the-classifier

After training has completed, the model's performance is estimated and displayed. The Custom Vision Service uses the images that you submitted for training to calculate precision and recall. Precision and recall are two different measurements of the effectiveness of a classifier:

- Precision indicates the fraction of identified classifications that were correct. For example, if the model identified 100 images as dogs, and 99 of them were actually of dogs, then the precision would be 99%.

- Recall indicates the fraction of actual classifications that were correctly identified. For example, if there were actually 100 images of apples, and the model identified 80 as apples, the recall would be 80%.

Custom Vision provides three metrics regarding the performance of your model: precision, recall, and AP.

https://www.tallan.com/blog/2020/05/19/azure-custom-vision/

8) 1) b, 2) c

1: LargeFaceListID

LargeFaceList: Add a face to a specified large face list, up to 1,000,000 faces.

Note: Given query face's faceId, to search the similar-looking faces from a faceId array, a face list or a large face list. A "faceListId" is created by FaceList - Create containing persistedFaceIds that will not expire. And a "largeFaceListId" is created by LargeFaceList - Create containing persistedFaceIds that will also not expire.

Incorrect Answers:

Not "faceListId": Add a face to a specified face list, up to 1,000 faces.

2: matchFace

Find similar has two working modes, "matchPerson" and "matchFace". "matchPerson" is the default mode that it tries to find faces of the same person as possible by using internal same-person thresholds. It is useful to find a known person's other photos. Note that an empty list will be returned if no faces pass the internal thresholds. "matchFace" mode ignores same-person thresholds and returns ranked similar faces anyway, even the similarity is low. It can be used in the cases like searching celebrity-looking faces.

It says "The call must find similar faces from an existing list named employeefaces", similar being the keyword here so matchFace is correct.

Reference:

https://docs.microsoft.com/en-us/rest/api/faceapi/face/findsimilar

https://learn.microsoft.com/en-us/rest/api/faceapi/face-list?
view=rest-faceapi-v1.0

9) Yes, Yes, No

x Left-coordinate of the top left point of the area, in pixels.

y Top-coordinate of the top left point of the area, in pixels.

w Width measured from the top-left point of the area, in pixels.

h Height measured from the top-left point of the area, in pixels.

2: Yes: Coordinates of a rectangle in the API refer to the top left corner.

3: No: the response returns Width and Height, which can be used to calculate the coordinates of bottom right corner, but it does not include them directly.

Reference:

https://learn.microsoft.com/en-us/azure/ai-services/
computer-vision/how-to/shelf-analyze#bounding-box-api-
model

10) [1] b, [2] a

[1] b. Stream

The File.OpenRead(String) method opens an existing file for reading.

Example: Open the stream and read it back.

using (FileStream fs = File.OpenRead(path))

[2] a. AddFaceFromStreamAsync

File.OpenRead() returns a Stream object.

```
using (Stream stream = File.OpenRead(imagePath))
{
await
faceClient.PersonGroupPerson.AddFaceFromStreamAsync(pers
onGroupId, personId, stream);
}
```

Reference:

literally the same code from Step 5 at https://docs.microsoft.com/en-us/azure/cognitive-services/face/face-api-how-to-topics/how-to-add-faces)

11) A

a. Multiclass.

Multilabel classification applies any number of tags to an image (zero or more), while multiclass classification sorts images into single categories (every image you submit will be sorted into the most likely tag). Therefore, using multilabel means that one image can be tagged as both "cat" and "dog" at the same time, although it should be either/or.

References:

https://learn.microsoft.com/en-us/azure/ai-services/custom-vision-service/getting-started-build-a-classifier

https://learn.microsoft.com/en-us/training/modules/classify-images/

12) A

The correct code to use for creating a free Azure resource in the West US region, to be used for automatic image caption generation, is:

A. create_resource("res1", "ComputerVision", "F0", "westus")

Explanation:

The "F0" SKU (Free Tier) is appropriate for a free Azure resource.

The "westus" location aligns with the requirement for the West US Azure region.

The "ComputerVision" kind indicates that the resource is intended for computer vision services, which is suitable for the automatic generation of image captions.

Computer vision provide automatic vision solutions including captions. The key-phrase is "automatic".

Reference:

https://learn.microsoft.com/en-us/azure/cognitive-services/cognitive-services-apis-create-account-client-library?pivots=programming-language-python#create-a-cognitive-services-resource-python

To create and subscribe to a new Cognitive Services resource, use the Create function. This function adds a new billable resource to the resource group you pass in. When you create your new resource, you'll need to know the "kind" of service you want to use, along with its pricing tier (or SKU) and an Azure location. The following function takes all of these arguments and creates a resource.

13) B

B. No

Explanation:

The provided solution suggests adding new images and then using the Smart Labeler tool. However, it doesn't mention the crucial steps of assigning labels to the new images and retraining the model. The Smart Labeler tool is helpful for suggesting labels based on the content of the images, but it doesn't replace the need for manual labeling and model retraining.

To meet the goal of incorporating new images into the classifier, the correct steps include:

Adding the new images.

Manually assigning labels to the new images.

Retraining the Custom Vision model with the updated dataset.

The provided solution is incomplete and does not fully address the necessary steps for successful model training.

The model needs to be extended and retrained.

Note: Smart Labeler to generate suggested tags for images. This lets you label a large number of images more quickly when training a Custom Vision model.

Reference:

https://learn.microsoft.com/en-us/azure/cognitive-services/custom-vision-service/suggested-tags

Smart Labeler will generate suggested tags for images. This lets you label a large number of images more quickly when you're training a Custom Vision model.

When you tag images for a Custom Vision model, the service uses the latest trained iteration of the model to predict the labels of new images. It shows these predictions as suggested tags, based on the selected confidence threshold and prediction uncertainty. You can then either confirm or change the suggestions, speeding up the process of manually tagging the images for training.

14) 1) c, 2) c

1.   https://westus.api.cognitive.microsoft.com/vision/v3.2/analyze/?visualFeatures=Adult,Description

2.   https://westus.api.cognitive.microsoft.com/vision/v3.2/analyze/?visualFeatures=Adult,Description

https://learn.microsoft.com/en-us/azure/cognitive-services/computer-vision/concept-describing-images

Computer Vision can analyze an image and generate a human-readable phrase that describes its contents. The algorithm returns several descriptions based on different visual features, and each description is given a confidence score. The final output is a list of descriptions ordered from highest to lowest confidence.

15) B

B. Host the Computer Vision endpoint in a container on an on-premises server.

Three primary parameters for all Cognitive Services containers

EXAM AI-102: DESIGNING AND IMPLEMENTING A MICROSOFT AZURE AI SO...

are required. The Microsoft Software License Terms must be present with a value of accept. An

Endpoint URI and API key are also needed.

Incorrect:

Not D: This Computer Vision endpoint would be available for the public, unless it is secured.

Reference:

https://docs.microsoft.com/en-us/azure/cognitive-services/computer-vision/deploy-computer-vision-on-premises

https://learn.microsoft.com/en-us/azure/cognitive-services/computer-vision/deploy-computer-vision-on-premises

One option to manage your Computer Vision containers on-premises is to use Kubernetes and Helm. Using Kubernetes and Helm to define a Computer Vision container image, we'll create a Kubernetes package. This package will be deployed to a Kubernetes cluster on-premises.

17) B

B. Optical Character Recognition (OCR)

Explanation:

To enable queries on the contents of handwritten letters, you should include the Optical Character Recognition (OCR) skill in the indexer. OCR skill extracts text from images, making the textual content of the letters searchable in the Azure Cognitive Search solution.

Options A, C, and D are not directly relevant to extracting text from images. Image analysis focuses on visual features, key phrase extraction identifies important phrases within text, and document extraction is more related to extracting structured information from documents rather than handwritten images.

To ensure that queries can be performed on the contents of the letters, the skill that should be included in the indexer is optical character recognition (OCR).

Option B, optical character recognition (OCR), is a technology that can recognize text within an image and convert it into machine-readable text. This skill will enable the search engine to read the handwritten letters and convert them into searchable text that can be indexed by Azure Cognitive Search.

Option A, image analysis, is a useful skill for analyzing images to extract metadata, but it does not directly enable text recognition.

Option C, key phrase extraction, extracts important phrases and concepts from text, but it requires the text to be already recognized and extracted by OCR or other text extraction techniques.

Option D, document extraction, is a skill that extracts specific pieces of information from documents, but it does not address the challenge of recognizing and extracting text from handwritten letters.

Reference:

https://learn.microsoft.com/en-us/azure/search/cognitive-search-skill-ocr

The Optical character recognition (OCR) skill recognizes printed and handwritten text in image files.

17)

1: a. Computer Vision analyze image

2: c. imageType

Service endpoint:

a. Computer Vision analyze images

Explanation: The "analyze images" endpoint of the Computer Vision service is suitable for a variety of image analysis tasks, including extracting information about the content of images.

Property:

c. imageType

Explanation: The imageType property, although not a native property of the Computer Vision service, is commonly used to categorize images into types such as photographs, drawings, or clipart. The availability of this property might depend on the specific version of the API or updates to the Computer Vision service.

Reference:

https://learn.microsoft.com/en-us/azure/cognitive-services/computer-vision/concept-detecting-image-types

With the Analyze Image API, Computer Vision can analyze the content type of images, indicating whether an image is clip art or a line drawing.

18) B

B. Call the face detection API repeatedly and check for changes to the FaceAttributes.HeadPose attribute.

You can detect head gestures like nodding and head shaking by tracking HeadPose changes in real time. You can use this feature as a custom liveness detector.

Liveness detection is the task of determining that a subject is a real person and not an image or video representation. A head gesture detector could serve as one way to help verify liveness, especially as opposed to an image representation of a person.

Reference:

https://learn.microsoft.com/en-us/azure/cognitive-services/computer-vision/how-to/use-headpose#detect-head-gestures

19) A

a. custom brands.

The Custom Brands model supports brand detection from speech and visuals.

Slate detection is used for clapper boards and digital patterns with color bars, and the custom Language model is used to add words that are not in the model.

To identify images and references related to competing companies in the Microsoft Teams meeting recordings, you should use the "custom brands" content model. This model allows you to define and train the system to recognize specific brands or entities of interest, aligning with the goal of identifying mentions and images related to competing companies.

References:

https://learn.microsoft.com/en-us/azure/azure-video-indexer/customize-brands-model-overview

https://learn.microsoft.com/en-us/training/modules/analyze-video/

20) A

To minimize the time required for index construction for the scanned documents and images in your Azure Storage account with an existing AI enrichment pipeline in Azure Cognitive Search, you should consider the following:

A. From the Azure portal, configure parallel indexing.

Explanation:

Parallel indexing involves splitting the indexing process into parallel tasks, allowing for faster processing of large datasets. Configuring parallel indexing in the Azure portal can significantly reduce the time required to build the index, especially when dealing with a substantial amount of data.

Options B, C, and D are less directly related to optimizing the indexing process for efficiency. Parallel indexing is a mechanism designed to handle large volumes of data more swiftly and is particularly relevant in scenarios where time efficiency is crucial.

Reference:

https://learn.microsoft.com/en-us/azure/search/search-howto-large-index#run-indexers-in-parallel

If you partition your data, you can create multiple indexer-data-source combinations that pull from each data source and write to the same search index. Because each indexer is distinct, you can run them at the same time, populating a search index more quickly than if you ran them sequentially.

21) 1) e, 2) f, 3) b

1) Sign in to the Azure Video Analyzer for Media website. (e)

2) From Content model customization, select Brands. (f)

3) Add the specific company names to the include list. (b)

Explanation:

Start by signing in to the Azure Video Analyzer for Media website to access the necessary tools and features.

In the Content model customization section, select Brands to configure the model specifically for identifying company names.

Add the specific company names to the include list to instruct the model to focus on detecting those particular entities during the analysis.

Reference:

https://learn.microsoft.com/en-us/azure/azure-video-indexer/customize-brands-model-with-website

22) A

To comply with regulations and directly transmit images of forms to the Form Recognizer API endpoint without storing them in the cloud, you should send the images in the raw image binary format.

Answer: A. raw image binary

Explanation:

Sending the images in raw image binary format allows you to transmit the image data directly to the Form Recognizer API without the need for storing the images in the cloud. This method enhances privacy and compliance with regulations by avoiding unnecessary data storage.

Options B (form URL encoded) and C (JSON) are not typically used for sending raw image data directly. Instead, they may be more suitable for other types of data or information exchange, but for sending image data, the raw image binary format is the appropriate choice.

References:

https://westus.dev.cognitive.microsoft.com/docs/services/form-recognizer-api-v2-1/operations/AnalyzeReceiptAsync

Request body: Document containing the receipt image(s) to be analyzed. The POST body should be the raw image binary, or the image URL in JSON.

https://ittichaicham.com/2020/03/call-azure-form-recognizer-api-on-sharepoint-document-image-url-in-power-automate/

Power Automate (formerly Microsoft Flow) can call Azure Form Recognizer via the connector. Since Power Automate is a cloud solution, the natural choice is to use the image URL. This should work fine if the URL is accessible to the public or requires no authentication. Unfortunately, the company's SharePoint URL, most of the time, is not.

To solve this, we can add another flow step to move the SharePoint file to where it is accessible, or, better, instead of using file URL, we can pass binary content in the Form Recognizer API.

23) C

C. Computer Vision Image Analysis.

Multilingual Tag Generation: Azure's Computer Vision Image Analysis service can analyze images and provide a list of tags describing the content of the images. It also has the capability to return these tags in various languages, including English, French, and Spanish, which aligns with your requirement.

Minimizing Development Effort: This service offers a pre-built model, which means there is no need for you to collect data and train your own model. This significantly reduces the development effort and time. You simply need to call the API with your images, and it will return the tags.

C is correct, because of the minimized development effort. Since the prebuilt model of C also fits the other two requirements, so there is no need to train a custom model.

References:

https://learn.microsoft.com/en-us/azure/cognitive-services/computer-vision/how-to/call-analyze-image?tabs=rest

https://learn.microsoft.com/en-us/azure/cognitive-services/computer-vision/concept-tagging-images

Image Analysis can return content tags for thousands of recognizable objects, living beings, scenery, and actions that appear in images. Tags are not organized as a taxonomy and do not have inheritance hierarchies. A collection of content tags forms the foundation for an image description displayed as human readable language formatted in complete sentences.

When tags are ambiguous or not common knowledge, the API response provides hints to clarify the meaning of the tag in context of a known setting.

https://learn.microsoft.com/en-us/azure/cognitive-services/ computer-vision/language-support#image-analysis

Some features of the Analyze - Image API can return results in other languages, specified with the language query parameter. Other actions return results in English regardless of what language is specified, and others throw an exception for unsupported languages. Actions are specified with the visual Features and details query parameters; see the Overview for a list of all the actions you can do with image analysis. Languages for tagging are only available in API version 3.2 or later.

24) B

B. No

Instead, you need to add the new images and labels to the existing model. You retrain the model, and then publish the model.

No need to create a new model, the existing one should be extended and retrained.

Note: Use Smart Labeler to generate suggested tags for images. This lets you label a large number of images more quickly when training a Custom Vision model.

Reference:

By limitation of the smart labeler: You should only request suggested tags for images whose tags have already been trained on once. Don't get suggestions for a new tag that you're just beginning to train. You are given new images of species that have not been seen by the model how can you expect it to suggest what they are? Also, you can train the model right in the smart labeler: check the workflow and the limitations in the doc.

https://learn.microsoft.com/en-us/azure/ai-services/custom-vision-service/suggested-tags

25) 1) f, 2) c

1. Object detection

2. General (compact)

Project type: Object detection (f) - Object detection is suitable for identifying and locating defects in packaging, allowing the model to outline specific regions of interest within an image.

Domain: General (compact) (c) - The General (compact) domain provides a balanced model suitable for various image analysis tasks, including object detection.

References:

These choices will help you develop a Custom Vision model capable of detecting defects in packaging and providing defect locations to an operator while ensuring the presence of four products in each package.

https://learn.microsoft.com/en-us/azure/cognitive-services/custom-vision-service/get-started-build-detector

- Select Object Detection under Project Types.

https://learn.microsoft.com/en-us/azure/cognitive-services/custom-vision-service/select-domain#compact-domains

The models generated by compact domains can be exported to run locally.

26) 1) a, 2) b

1. 0

2. 25

https://learn.microsoft.com/en-us/azure/cognitive-services/ language-service/custom-text-classification/concepts/ evaluation-metrics

- Precision: Measures how precise/accurate your model is. It's the ratio between the correctly identified positives (true positives) and all identified positives. The precision metric reveals how many of the predicted classes are correctly labeled.

Precision = #True_Positive / (#True_Positive + #False_Positive)

- Recall: Measures the model's ability to predict actual positive classes. It's the ratio between the predicted true positives and what was actually tagged. The recall metric reveals how many of the predicted classes are correct.

Recall = #True_Positive / (#True_Positive + #False_Negatives)

27) B

To configure the app to extract text from images while minimizing development effort for one million scanned magazine articles stored as image files, you should include:

B. The Read API in Computer Vision

Explanation:

The Read API in Computer Vision is specifically designed for extracting text from images. It can analyze the content of images, including scanned documents and articles, and extract text information.

Option A (Computer Vision Image Analysis) is a broader option that includes various image analysis capabilities, but for text extraction, the Read API is more specific and efficient.

Options C (Form Recognizer) and D (Azure Cognitive Service for Language) are not as directly tailored for extracting text from images as the Read API in Computer Vision, which is designed for this specific task.

References:

Use this interface to get the result of a Read operation, employing the state-of-the-art Optical Character Recognition (OCR) algorithms optimized for text-heavy documents.

https://learn.microsoft.com/en-us/rest/api/
computervision/3.2preview2/read/read?tabs=HTTP

B. With the new Image Analysis API 4.0 (in preview) you could use OCR feature too, but as we said, it is in preview.

https://learn.microsoft.com/en-us/azure/ai-services/
computer-vision/overview-image-analysis?tabs=4-0

Instead, the Read API is particularly adapted for text-heavy documents and it seems this is the case

https://learn.microsoft.com/en-us/rest/api/computervision/
read/read?view=rest-computervision-v3.1&tabs=HTTP

28) C

C. Upload File1.avi to Microsoft OneDrive.

When uploading videos consider using a URL over byte array.

Azure AI Video Indexer does give you the choice to upload videos from URL or directly by sending the file as a byte array, the latter comes with some constraints. For more information, see uploading considerations and limitations)

First, it has file size limitations. The size of the byte array file is limited to 2 GB compared to the 30-GB upload size limitation while using URL.

Uploading Guidelines:

Uploading files to Video Indexer

Uploading a local file from your device

Supported file formats include: .wmv, .avi, .mov.

The file should be up to 2GB and up to 4 hours.

You can upload up to 10 files at a time.

Uploading an online file

The URL should lead to an online media file (for example a OneDrive file),

not a webpage (like www.youtube.com).

The file should be up to 30GB and up to 4 hours.

You can upload up to 10 files at a time.

Reference:

https://learn.microsoft.com/it-it/azure/azure-video-indexer/
considerations-when-use-at-scale

Note: This question is part of free assessment given by Microsoft
and the answer in that is C.

29) A

A. Yes

It's important to note that the effectiveness of using patterns
or examples may depend on the specific requirements and
variations in user input. If you have confidence that the pattern
alone is suitable for capturing the intended user queries, then A.
Yes, would be the correct choice.

Using a pattern could be a good solution IMHO...

∞ Find contacts in London.

∞ Who do I know in Seattle?

∞ Search for contacts in Ukraine.

Like

Where is {FormName}[?]

Who authored {FormName}[?]

{FormName} is published in French[?]

(taken from https://docs.microsoft.com/en-us/azure/cognitive-
services/luis/luis-concept-patterns)

we could do:

∞ Find contacts in {CityOrCountry}.

∞ Who do I know in {CityOrCountry}[?]

∞ Search for contacts in {CityOrCountry}[?].

Reference:

https://www.examtopics.com/exams/microsoft/ai-102/view/19/#:~:text=According%20to%20MS%20learn%2C%20answer%20should%20be%20yes%20(A)%0A%0Ahttps%3A//learn.microsoft.com/en%2Dus/training/modules/create%2Dlanguage%2Dunderstanding%2Dapp/5%2Duse%2Dpatterns%2Dto%2Ddifferentiate%2Dsimilar%2Dutterances%0A%0AThis%20is%20a%20FindContact%20intent%20with%20a%20location%20entity%20pattern

30) A

A. Yes

Explanation:

The provided solution correctly outlines the steps required to incorporate new images into a Custom Vision model:

Add the new images and labels to the existing model.

Retrain the model with the updated dataset.

Publish the updated model.

This process ensures that the model learns from the new images and their associated labels, improving its ability to recognize different flower species. Therefore, the goal is met with the provided solution.

Uploading, tagging, retraining and publishing the model.

Instead, the model needs to be extended and retrained.

Note: Use Smart Labeler to generate suggested tags for images. This lets you label a large number of images more quickly when training a Custom Vision model.

31) 1) b, 2) d

1: {"fr", "de", "es"}

A common task of speech translation is to specify target translation languages, at least one is required but multiples are supported. The following code snippet sets both French and German as translation language targets. static async Task TranslateSpeechAsync()

{

var translationConfig =

SpeechTranslationConfig.FromSubscription(SPEECH_SUBSCRIPTION_KEY, SPEECH_SERVICE_REGION); translationConfig.SpeechRecognitionLanguage = "it-IT";

// Translate to languages. See, https://aka.ms/speech/stttlanguages translationConfig.AddTargetLanguage("fr"); translationConfig.AddTargetLanguage("de");

}

2: TranslationRecognizer

After you've created a SpeechTranslationConfig, the next step is to initialize a TranslationRecognizer.

Example code:

```
static async Task TranslateSpeechAsync()
{
var translationConfig =
SpeechTranslationConfig.FromSubscription(SPEECH_SUBSCRIPTION_KEY, SPEECH_SERVICE_REGION); var fromLanguage = "en-US"; var toLanguages = new List<string> { "it", "fr", "de" };
translationConfig.SpeechRecognitionLanguage = fromLanguage;
toLanguages.ForEach(translationConfig.AddTargetLanguage);
using var recognizer = new TranslationRecognizer(translationConfig);
}
```

Reference:

https://docs.microsoft.com/en-us/dotnet/api/
microsoft.cognitiveservices.speech.translation.translationreco
gnizer?view=azure-dotnet

32) 1) d, 2) a, 3) e

d. Group the images locally into category folders.

a. Upload the images by category.

e. Review the suggestions and confirm the tags.

Explanation:

Grouping the images locally into category folders helps organize them effectively before uploading.

Uploading the images by category ensures that the data is structured and facilitates a more organized training process.

Reviewing the suggested tags and confirming them helps in validating and refining the tagging process for the training images.

The question emphasizes two things: 1) the model has already been trained. 2) the solution should be expedient.

Reference:

https://docs.microsoft.com/en-us/azure/cognitive-services/custom-vision-service/suggested-tags

33) A

For capturing billing addresses in a Conversational Language Understanding model for an e-commerce chatbot, the most appropriate entity type is:

A. Machine Learned

Explanation:

Machine Learned entities are well-suited for handling complex and varied patterns in user input, such as billing addresses, as they can adapt and generalize from examples.

Billing addresses can have diverse formats, and a machine learned entity is capable of recognizing and extracting such variations.

Regex (B) might be too rigid for capturing the variability in billing addresses, and Pattern.any (D) may not provide the necessary precision for structured data like addresses.

EXAM AI-102: DESIGNING AND IMPLEMENTING A MICROSOFT AZURE AI SO...

Lists (C) could be used for specific predefined values but may not cover the flexibility needed for billing addresses.

Therefore, using a machine-learned entity is the most appropriate choice for capturing billing addresses.

Reference:

https://learn.microsoft.com/en-us/azure/cognitive-services/LUIS/concepts/entities#ml-entity-with-structure

- ML Entity with Structure

An ML entity can be composed of smaller sub-entities, each of which can have its own properties. For example, an Address entity could have the following structure:

Address: 4567 Main Street, NY, 98052, USA

Building Number: 4567

Street Name: Main Street

State: NY

Zip Code: 98052

Country: USA

34) BD

The correct actions to include in the method are:

B. Call the client.Knowledgebase.CreateAsync method.

D. Create a CreateKbDTO object.

Explanation:

B. To initiate the creation of knowledge bases, you need to call the appropriate method from the QnAMakerClient, which is CreateAsync in this case.

D. You should create a CreateKbDTO object to provide the necessary data and configuration for creating knowledge bases. This object typically includes information such as Q&A pairs, URLs, and other relevant settings.

Options A and C involve creating lists of objects representing data from the WebJob, but they are not directly related to the specific actions required to initiate the creation of knowledge bases in the QnAMakerClient.

Extra explanation:

A. Create a list of FileDTO objects that represents data from the WebJob.

NO - as it is from URL - so optional

B. Call the client.Knowledgebase.CreateAsync method.

YES - Mandatory to Call the Method

C. Create a list of QnADTO objects that represents data from the WebJob.

NO - as it is from URL - so optional

D. Create a CreateKbDTO object.

YES - Mandatory to Create

Go through the lines starting line 92 at below URL:

https://github.com/Azure-Samples/cognitive-services-qnamaker-csharp/blob/master/documentation-samples/quickstarts/Knowledgebase_Quickstart/Program.cs

Reference:

https://docs.microsoft.com/en-us/azure/cognitive-services/qnamaker/quickstarts/quickstart-sdk?tabs=v1%2Cversion-1&pivots=programming-language-csharp

35) 1) e, 2) c

1. api-nam.cognitive.microsofttranslator.com

2. var uri= endpoint +"?to=en";

References:

https://learn.microsoft.com/en-us/azure/cognitive-services/Translator/reference/v3-0-reference#base-urls

Requests to Translator are, in most cases, handled by the datacenter that is closest to where the request originated. If there's a datacenter failure when using the global endpoint, the request may be routed outside of the geography.

To force the request to be handled within a specific geography, use the desired geographical endpoint. All requests are processed among the datacenters within the geography.

- United States

api-nam.cognitive.microsofttranslator.com

https://learn.microsoft.com/en-us/azure/cognitive-services/translator/reference/rest-api-guide

- translate

Translate specified source language text into the target language text.

36) C

The correct option for enabling active learning is:

C. Add log=true to the prediction endpoint query.

Explanation:

Active learning involves continuously improving the language understanding model by learning from user interactions and feedback. By adding log=true to the prediction endpoint query, you enable logging of user interactions. This logged data can be utilized for model retraining, incorporating new insights and improving the model's performance over time.

Options A, B, and D do not directly address active learning. Option A is related to showing all intents in predictions, option B refers to speech priming, and option D involves sentiment analysis, which is not directly linked to active learning in the context of improving language understanding through user interactions.

Reference:

"To enable active learning, you must log user queries. This is accomplished by calling the endpoint query with the log=true query string parameter and value."

https://docs.microsoft.com/en-us/azure/cognitive-services/ LUIS/how-to/improve-application#log-user-queries-to-enable- active-learning

37) Yes, No, Yes

Explanation:

Yes - Going to http://localhost:5000/status is a common convention for checking the health status or availability of a service. In this context, it would query the Azure endpoint to verify the validity of the API key used to start the container.

Typically, Azure Cognitive Services containers provide a /status endpoint that can be used to check the status of the service, including the validity of the API key. Since the service is mapped to localhost:5000, accessing this URL should provide the status of the containerized service, including the API key's validity. The container logging provider will write log data.

No - The provided command does not include any specific configuration for logging. Whether the container logging provider writes log data depends on the default settings or any additional configuration that is not visible in the given command.

Log location is not mounted. The ET answer relates to an example provided on the given website which DOES mount a log location.

Yes - Going to http://localhost:5000/swagger is a common convention for accessing Swagger documentation, which provides details about the available endpoints and how to interact with them.

Reference:

https://learn.microsoft.com/en-us/azure/cognitive-services/language-service/text-analytics-for-health/how-to/use-containers?tabs=language#validate-that-a-container-is-running

38) A

For capturing billing addresses in a Language Understanding model for an e-commerce platform, the most suitable entity type is:

A. Machine Learned

Explanation:

Machine Learned entities are well-suited for handling complex and varied patterns in user input, such as billing addresses, as they can adapt and generalize from examples.

Billing addresses can have diverse formats, and a machine learned entity is capable of recognizing and extracting such variations.

Regex (B) might be too rigid for capturing the variability in billing addresses, geographyV2 (C) is designed for geographical entities and might not capture all the nuances of a billing address, and Pattern.any (D) may not provide the necessary precision for structured data like addresses.

Lists (E) could be used for specific predefined values but may not cover the flexibility needed for billing addresses.

Therefore, using a machine-learned entity is the most appropriate choice for capturing billing addresses.

An ML entity can be composed of smaller sub-entities, each of which can have its own properties. For example, Address could have the following structure:

Address: 4567 Main Street, NY, 98052, USA

Building Number: 4567

Street Name: Main Street

State: NY

Zip Code: 98052

Country: USA

Reference:

https://docs.microsoft.com/en-us/azure/cognitive-services/luis/luis-concept-entity-types

It is a Machine Learned Entity (check ML Entity with Structure in the link, as it is an Address example...)

39) C, D, F

The correct combination of three additional query parameters to achieve the desired translation of content into Greek with a transliteration in the Roman alphabet is:

C. textType=html - Specifies that the content to be translated is in HTML format.

D. to=el - Specifies the target language as Greek.

F. toScript=Latn - Specifies the transliteration script as Latin (Roman alphabet).

Explanation:

C. textType=html - This parameter specifies that the content being provided for translation is in HTML format. It's crucial to include this when dealing with web page content as it informs the Translator API about the type of text, allowing it to handle HTML tags appropriately during translation.

D. to=el - This parameter sets the target language for translation as Greek (el). It instructs the Translator API to translate the content into the Greek language.

F. toScript=Latn - This parameter specifies the transliteration script as Latin (Latn), which corresponds to the Roman alphabet. Including this ensures that, in addition to the translation, you also receive a transliteration of the Greek text using the Roman alphabet.

In summary, these three parameters collectively instruct the Translator API to translate HTML-formatted content from the source language to Greek while providing a transliteration in the Roman alphabet.

References:

https://docs.microsoft.com/en-us/azure/cognitive-services/translator/reference/v3-0-translate#translate-with-transliteration

https://api.cognitive.microsofttranslator.com/translate?api-version=3.0&textType=html&to=el&toScript=Latn

40) C, E

C. Bot Framework Emulator: This is an essential tool for debugging Microsoft Bot Framework bots. It allows you to test and debug your bots on your local machine by emulating the Bot Framework's channels and activities. It can be very helpful in a local development environment but is less suited for remote debugging.

E. ngrok: ngrok is a tool that creates a secure tunnel to your localhost. This is very useful for remote debugging because it allows you to expose your local development server to the internet, which is necessary for testing and debugging interactions with services like the Microsoft Bot Framework.

To conduct remote debugging on the endpoint of a chatbot created with the Microsoft Bot Framework, installing Bot Framework Emulator (C) and ngrok (E) on your local computer is indeed the appropriate solution.

Bot Framework Emulator (C) allows you to test and debug your bot locally by simulating the conversation with the bot. It provides a user interface for interacting with your bot and inspecting the messages exchanged.

ngrok (E) helps in creating secure tunnels to your local machine, enabling your locally hosted bot endpoint to be accessible from the internet. This is crucial for remote debugging scenarios.

By using these tools together, you can efficiently debug and test your bot's functionality both locally and remotely.

Reference:

https://learn.microsoft.com/en-us/azure/bot-service/bot-service-debug-channel-ngrok?view=azure-bot-service-4.0

41) 1) e, 2) b, 3) d

1: Add alternative phrasing to the question and answer (QnA) pair.

Add alternate questions to an existing QnA pair to improve the likelihood of a match to a user query.

2: Retrain the model.

Periodically select Save and train after making edits to avoid losing changes.

3: Republish the model.

Note: A knowledge base consists of question and answer (QnA) pairs. Each pair has one answer and a pair contains all the information associated with that answer.

Reference:

https://docs.microsoft.com/en-us/azure/cognitive-services/qnamaker/how-to/edit-knowledge-base

Reference:

https://learn.microsoft.com/en-us/azure/cognitive-services/qnamaker/how-to/edit-knowledge-base#question-and-answer-pairs

The optional settings for a pair include:

- Alternate forms of the question

this helps QnA Maker return the correct answer for a wider variety of question phrasings.

42) B

B. No

Explanation:

Creating a new intent for location does not directly align with the goal of implementing the provided phrase list within Language Understanding for the FindContact intent. The phrases are intended for searching contacts, and the relevant concept in this context is finding contacts, not specifically the location.

To meet the goal, you should create or use the existing intent labeled FindContact and train the model with the provided phrases, focusing on identifying user intent related to finding contacts rather than creating a new intent for location.

Reference:

An utterance having wo intents? This is illogical.

The model should have an Entity "Location" that will help in finding the contacts.

The intent is for FindContact, not location really.

https://docs.microsoft.com/en-us/azure/cognitive-services/luis/luis-concept-intent

43) D

D. Add examples to the None intent.

The correct option to decrease the likelihood of a false positive in the Language Understanding model is to add additional None intent examples.

Option D is correct. By adding more varied examples that do not map to a valid intent to the None intent, the model can better learn when an utterance does not apply and avoid falsely matching invalid queries to a valid intent.

Options A, B, and C may improve the model in certain ways, but they do not directly address reducing false positives. Only adding additional out-of-scope examples to the None intent will help the model better distinguish when new utterances do not match any existing intent's patterns.

So out of the options, adding examples to the None intent is the way to decrease the likelihood of false positives.

You should also consider adding false positive examples to the None intent. For example, in a flight booking project it is likely that the utterance "I want to buy a book" could be confused with a Book Flight intent. Adding "I want to buy a book" or "I love reading books" as None training utterances helps alter the predictions of those types of utterances towards the None intent instead of Book Flight.

https://learn.microsoft.com/en-us/azure/cognitive-services/language-service/conversational-language-understanding/concepts/none-intent#adding-examples-to-the-none-intent

"You should also consider adding false positive examples to the None intent."

44) 1) d, 2) a, 3) e

Paris: d. GeographyV2

email@domain.com: a. Email

2 audit business: e. Machine learned

Explanation:

Paris: The location "Paris" can be effectively captured using the built-in entity type for geography, which is GeographyV2.

email@domain.com: The email address "email@domain.com" can be accurately recognized using the built-in entity type for emails, which is Email.

2 audit business: The phrase "2 audit business" appears to be specific and not a standard or predefined format. Hence, a machine-learned entity type would be appropriate for capturing this information, as it may not fit into a predefined list or

pattern.

Extra explanation:

1: GeographyV2:

The prebuilt geographyV2 entity detects places. Because this entity is already trained, you do not need to add example utterances containing GeographyV2 to the application intents.

2: Email:

Email prebuilt entity for a LUIS app: Email extraction includes the entire email address from an utterance. Because this entity is already trained, you do not need to add example utterances containing email to the application intents.

3: Machine learned:

The machine-learning entity is the preferred entity for building LUIS applications.

References:

Geography v2:

https://docs.microsoft.com/en-us/azure/cognitive-services/luis/luis-reference-prebuilt-geographyv2?tabs=V3

Email:

https://docs.microsoft.com/en-us/azure/cognitive-services/luis/luis-reference-prebuilt-email?tabs=V3-verbose

Machine Learned:

https://docs.microsoft.com/en-us/azure/cognitive-services/luis/reference-entity-machine-learned-entity?tabs=V3

https://docs.microsoft.com/en-us/azure/cognitive-services/luis/concepts/entities

45) D

d. waterfall

The waterfall dialog defines a sequence of steps, allowing your bot to guide a user through a linear process. These are typically designed to work within the context of a component dialog.

The action dialog supports the implementation of actions in Composer and the question and AskUser dialogs are unavailable in this case.

In the context of the Microsoft Bot Framework SDK, a waterfall dialog is a type of dialog that allows you to prompt the user for information in a predefined order. It consists of a sequence of steps or prompts, where the output of one step can be used as input for the next step. Each step in the waterfall is implemented as a function, and the dialog proceeds through these steps in a linear order.

This type of dialog is well-suited for scenarios where you want to guide users through a series of questions or prompts, ensuring a structured conversation flow. The waterfall dialog simplifies the process of managing the conversation and collecting information from users in a systematic manner.

References:

https://learn.microsoft.com/en-us/azure/bot-service/bot-builder-concept-dialog?view=azure-bot-service-4.0

https://learn.microsoft.com/en-us/training/modules/design-bot-conversation-flow/

46) A

In the provided JSON sample, the "Weather.Historic" entity corresponds to the expression "last year" in the utterance. Therefore, the correct answer is:

A. by month

47) B

B. Named Entity Recognition

Named Entity Recognition (NER) is a process in natural language processing that identifies and classifies named entities mentioned in text into predefined categories such as the names of persons, organizations, locations, expressions of times, quantities, monetary values, percentages, etc.

Entity Linking typically involves linking entities to knowledge bases.

Sentiment Analysis is used to determine the sentiment expressed in the text.

Key Phrase Extraction identifies the main points or topics in a text but does not categorize them into entity types like NER does.

Reference:

https://learn.microsoft.com/en-us/azure/cognitive-services/

language-service/named-entity-recognition/overview

Named Entity Recognition (NER) is one of the features offered by Azure Cognitive Service for Language, a collection of machine learning and AI algorithms in the cloud for developing intelligent applications that involve written language. The NER feature can identify and categorize entities in unstructured text. For example: people, places, organizations, and quantities.

48) C

To ensure that App1 includes more detailed information during the sentiment analysis, especially when it incorrectly identifies positive sentiments as negative, you should add:

c. opinionMining=true

Explanation:

Enabling opinion mining (option c) in the API requests will allow App1 to provide more granular information by extracting opinions and sentiments from the text. This can help in understanding the nuances within customer feedback and improve the accuracy of sentiment analysis.

Options a and b are not directly related to obtaining more detailed information about sentiment analysis in the context described.

opinionMining=true will add aspect-based sentiment analysis, which in turn will make the sentiment more granular so that positive and negative in a single sentence can be returned.

loggingOptOut=true will opt out of logging and StringIndexType=TextElements_v8 will set the returned offset and length values to correspond with TextElements.

49) B

Person and Address will detect names and addresses.

PersonType will also remove job roles. IP will also remove IP addresses.

50) C

For an application that aims to identify documents containing the names of staff members using the Azure AI Language Personally Identifiable Information (PII) detection feature, the appropriate category to use is:

c. Person

The Person category detects names of people in the PII detection feature. The PhoneNumber category detects phone numbers, the age category detects people's ages, and the DateTime detects dates and time values.

51) C

c. The best solution will depend on the specific case you must solve.

Explanation:

Handling user interactions in a bot can vary based on the specific use case and requirements. The appropriate approach may depend on factors such as the nature of the conversation, user preferences, and the overall design goals of the bot. It's essential to consider the context and tailor the handling of the situation accordingly.

For specific use cases, you might need a different solution. If the user orders a product and changes their mind, you need to reset the dialog stack and make them select a different product. If you need the user's delivery information to complete the order, it is best you complete the current query. If you reset the dialog stack, you can lose important information that the user might have already answered in some cases.

References:

https://learn.microsoft.com/en-us/azure/bot-service/bot-service-design-conversation-flow?view=azure-bot-service-4.0

https://learn.microsoft.com/en-us/training/modules/design-bot-conversation-flow/

52) A

a. Hello, I'm the bot responsible for your sock orders.

Explanation:

The suggested option (a) provides a clear and direct introduction, informing the user about the bot's purpose and responsibility in handling sock orders. It sets the tone for a specific and focused interaction related to the task at hand. This helps the user understand the bot's role and initiates the conversation in a way that aligns with the bot's purpose.

"Hello. I'm the bot responsible for your sock orders" is a good way to start a conversation. It clearly states what the bot is going to do.

"Hey, how can I help you?" is not a good way to start a conversation: It does not provide any clues about what the bot is expecting from the end user.

"Hello sir, I hope you are having a good day?" is not a good conversation starter, it is not clear what is expected from the end user.

References:

https://learn.microsoft.com/en-us/azure/bot-service/bot-service-design-first-interaction?view=azure-bot-service-4.0

https://learn.microsoft.com/en-us/training/modules/design-bot-conversation-flow/

53) B

b. conversation

Properties in the conversation scope have a lifetime of the conversation itself. These properties are in the scope while the bot is processing an activity associated with the conversation, whereas the other scopes offer different property lifetimes.

When developing a bot using Azure AI Bot Service and the Microsoft Bot Framework Composer, using the "conversation" scope is appropriate for storing information that should persist throughout the entire conversation session. The conversation scope ensures that the collected data is available and accessible for the duration of the interaction between the user and the bot. Once the conversation session concludes, the information stored in the conversation scope is automatically cleared, helping to maintain privacy and security by removing sensitive data after each session.

References:

https://learn.microsoft.com/en-us/composer/ref-memory-variables?tabs=v2x

https://learn.microsoft.com/en-us/training/modules/create-bot-with-bot-framework-composer/

54) A

a. turn.activity.locale

The turn.activity.locale prebuilt property holds the language code of the text field of a message sent by the user, whereas the other properties are not available in Composer.

References:

https://learn.microsoft.com/en-us/composer/ref-memory-variables?tabs=v2x

https://learn.microsoft.com/en-us/training/modules/create-bot-with-bot-framework-composer/

55) C

c. a trace activity

To perform interactive debugging using the Bot Framework Emulator, you should add a trace activity to the code. A trace activity is a message sent from the bot to the emulator for debugging purposes. It allows you to inspect the flow of conversation and check the state of the bot during runtime. By adding trace activities strategically in your code, you can gather information about the execution flow, variable values, and other relevant details to aid in debugging. This helps developers understand how the bot processes messages and responses, facilitating effective debugging and troubleshooting.

A trace activity is an activity that your bot can send to the Bot Framework Emulator. You can use trace activities to interactively debug a bot, as they allow you to view information about your bot while it runs locally.

Test dialog and mock dialog are used for unit testing.

References:

https://learn.microsoft.com/en-us/azure/bot-service/unit-test-bots?view=azure-bot-service-4.0&tabs=csharp

https://learn.microsoft.com/en-us/training/modules/create-bot-with-bot-framework-composer/

56) A

a. a multi-tenant app

When developing a bot that will serve both your organization and partner companies, you should use a multi-tenant app. A multi-tenant app allows users from different organizations (tenants) to sign in and use the application with their own credentials. It supports a scenario where users from multiple Azure Active Directory (Azure AD) tenants can authenticate and access the bot.

Using a multi-tenant app is suitable for scenarios where your bot needs to interact with users from various organizations, providing a more flexible and inclusive approach to user authentication and access.

A multi-tenant app is used for partner companies, and it needs to be multi-tenant.

A managed identity is limited to a single tenant, and single tenant is incorrect.

References:

https://learn.microsoft.com/en-us/azure/bot-service/provision-and-publish-a-bot?view=azure-bot-service-4.0&tabs=userassigned%2Ccsharp

https://learn.microsoft.com/en-us/training/modules/design-bot-conversation-flow/

58) B

b. https://chatbot.azurewebsites.net/api/messages

To test and debug the bot using the Bot Framework Emulator, you should use the URL: https://chatbot.azurewebsites.net/api/messages. This URL points to the endpoint where the Bot Framework Emulator can send messages to interact with your deployed bot on Azure. The /api/messages route is a common endpoint for receiving messages in a Bot Framework application. Using this URL ensures that the emulator can communicate with your bot and allows you to test and debug its behavior.

The messaging endpoint of every bot is https://FQDN/api/messages, so the only valid option is:

https://chatbot.azurewebsites.net/api/messages.

References:

https://learn.microsoft.com/en-us/azure/bot-service/bot-service-debug-emulator?view=azure-bot-service-4.0&tabs=csharp

https://learn.microsoft.com/en-us/training/modules/create-bot-with-bot-framework-composer/

58) C

c. practical development tips.

A Conversational User Experience (CUX) guide is a set of practical development tips that provide guidelines and best practices for creating a positive and effective user experience in a conversational interface. It typically includes recommendations on structuring dialogues, handling user inputs, managing context, and ensuring a smooth and natural interaction flow. The guide helps developers design conversations that are engaging, user-friendly, and aligned with the goals of the digital assistant or chatbot.

Practical development tips are correct. The CUX guide is divided loosely into a few different sections. The CUX guide includes an introduction to CUX, ethics and inclusive design, a brainstorming worksheet and guidelines for planning and designing, and practical development tips for building CUX experiences.

CSS and licensing are not in the CUX guide.

References:

https://learn.microsoft.com/en-us/azure/bot-service/bot-service-design-principles?view=azure-bot-service-4.0

https://learn.microsoft.com/en-us/training/modules/design-bot-conversation-flow/

59) B

b. the visible text in the image and a description of the image content.

The request will return the visible text in the image and a description of the image content. This is because the specified features are "read" and "description," indicating that both the visible text and a description of the image content will be included in the analysis results.

The features used in the call are read and description, which will return the visible text in the image, as well as a description of the image content.

To return the objects that are in the image and their approximate location, the feature used in the call should be objects. To return a description of the image content only, the feature description should be used alone.

References:

https://learn.microsoft.com/en-us/azure/ai-services/computer-vision/how-to/call-analyze-image?tabs=rest

https://learn.microsoft.com/en-us/training/modules/read-text-images-documents-with-computer-vision-service/

60) D

d. Spatial Analysis.

The only visual feature that provides this capability is Spatial Analysis, as OCR, Image Analysis, and face detection are not meant to analyze the presence of people in a video feed.

References:

https://learn.microsoft.com/en-us/azure/ai-services/computer-vision/overview

https://learn.microsoft.com/en-us/training/modules/analyze-video/

Feel free to contact me on LinkedIn at "Georgio Daccache" for any assistance or questions. I'll be happy to help at any time.

Good Luck!

www.ingramcontent.com/pod-product-compliance
Lightning Source LLC
La Vergne TN
LVHW051332050326
832903LV00031B/3489

*9 7 9 8 8 7 8 3 0 7 0 8 6 *